BRITAIN'S GROW

G000124101

AN A-Z GUIDE TO MORE THAN 400 I
SIXTH EDITION

A comprehensive listing of stations and railway lines opened and
reopened throughout Britain's rail network since 1960

Edited by Jerry Alderson and Ian McDonald
Based on contributions from members
of Railfuture and original work by Alan Bevan

railfuture

For additional copies of this book, email: books@railfuture.org.uk
or go to website: www.railfuture.org.uk

Printed by The Charlesworth Group, Flanshaw Way, Flanshaw Lane, Wakefield WF2 9LP

ISBN 978-0-901283-19-1

Front cover picture:

Tweedbank station on the Borders Railway opened in 2015 with a horseback welcome from Galashiels' Braw Lad Cameron Pate and Braw Lass Abbie Franklin By VISITSCOTLAND

Back cover picture:

Ilkeston station reopened in 2017. Schoolchildren designed posters and Chaucer Primary School pupils planted shrubs By EAST MIDLANDS TRAINS

Back cover picture:

**Local railway historian Brian Amos, Maggie Throup MP and Jake Kelly, managing director of East Midlands Trains
Ms Throup said: "We have finally cast off the dubious title of the largest town in Britain without a station"** By EAST MIDLANDS TRAINS

Introduction

Britain's railways offer immense potential to provide fast, safe, attractive public transport to relieve our congested, polluted and dangerous roads. They are also the most environmentally sustainable form of transport, other than cycling, vital now that both climate change and air pollution are recognised as real threats.

Britain has the fastest growing railway in Europe, as the rail industry and politicians keep telling us. They are, however, referring to ever-growing numbers of passengers rather than expansion of the rail network.

Now there is a real chance that the railways will be expanded. Coinciding with the publication of this book is a new guide *Expanding the Railways,* financed by the Department for Transport but produced by the Campaign for Better Transport in partnership with Railfuture. *Expanding the Railways* shows how reopening proposals and other schemes can be developed from an idea into a reality. There must be cooperation between campaigners, local authorities, local enterprise partnerships, train operators and property developers.

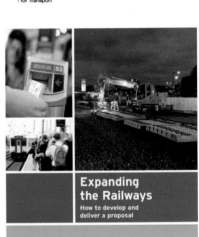

The guide explains in no-nonsense language how ideas must be subjected to rigorous examination before a business case can be developed, then support must be sought from as many different organisations as possible before sources of funding are identified which will allow the scheme to be delivered.

The guide includes many useful check questions which promoters of schemes must ask themselves. The mere presence of a disused track bed is not sufficient to justify the work needed to reintroduce a train service. However, housing growth near a line that closed 50 years ago may have transformed its financial prospects.

Expanding the Railways includes case studies to encourage campaigners to think positively. Technical details will be useful to Railfuture members and campaigners.

The implications of Transport & Works Act Orders, and the powers granted by such an Order are explained, as is the Guide to Rail Investment Process (GRIP) which railway projects must follow. Also explained is the four-stage Network Rail investment process, and the Department for Transport's model approach to investment decision making.

The 40-page *Expanding the Railways* is a must for all campaigners and can be viewed online at www.railfuture.org.uk/display1563. The guide was launched with a flourish at a gathering of transport planners and advocates of railway reopenings in the National Railway Museum at York on 5 July 2017.

At the launch, the Rail Delivery Group's *Passenger Demand Forecasting Handbook* was criticised for always underpredicting demand so new facilities such as the Borders Railway are built with inadequate facilities.

The Network Rail GRIP procedure was condemned as too long and too expensive, with each stage tending to take two years. This long-term approach is incompatible with soliciting developer contributions.

Despite the difficulties, new stations and new lines have been built, with most of the reopened stations seeing healthy growth in passenger numbers. To rail campaigners who remember the 1960s and 1970s, it seems almost miraculous. Back then the future seemed to belong to motorways and air travel, with the railway expected to decline. Not any more.

For most of the stations listed in this edition of *Britain's Growing Railways*, we can now quote the passenger usage figures published by the Office of Rail and Road in 2016. The 2017 figures will be available soon after this edition is published.

Passenger numbers keep growing

For example, Bicester Village station, which reopened in 2015, attracted more than 400,000 passengers in its first full year of operation. Aylesbury Vale Parkway station saw numbers grow by 40,000 over one year. Ebbsfleet International station in Kent saw passenger numbers grow by 200,000 in 2015, while at Stratford International numbers increased by more than half a million to 1,632,646. Both Stratford and Ebbsfleet are served by Javelin trains on Britain's first high speed line. Two stations on the North London line, Hackney Wick and Hackney Central, each had 270,000 extra passengers in 2016. Although some of this growth results from a change to a more accurate method of estimating passengers, it is worth remembering that Dr Beeching and some British Rail managers wanted to close this line in the 1960s.

In Scotland, Dunfermline Queen Margaret which reopened in 2000, saw passenger numbers grow by 25,000 in 2016.

Railfuture was set up to prevent further shrinking of the railway network. Now though, there is overwhelming public demand for travel by rail.

There is only so much growth that can be achieved by running longer trains, extending platforms, running more frequent services, increasing capacity through improved signalling to enable trains to run closer together, and upgrading routes.

The official view in Westminster, the Scottish Parliament, the Welsh Government and the English regions is that providing new stations and railway lines makes sense.

When new services are provided, the response from passengers often exceeds expectations. Put on a decent train service and people will use it!

This latest edition of the *Britain's Growing Railway* celebrates the success of many of our previous campaigns.

Contents

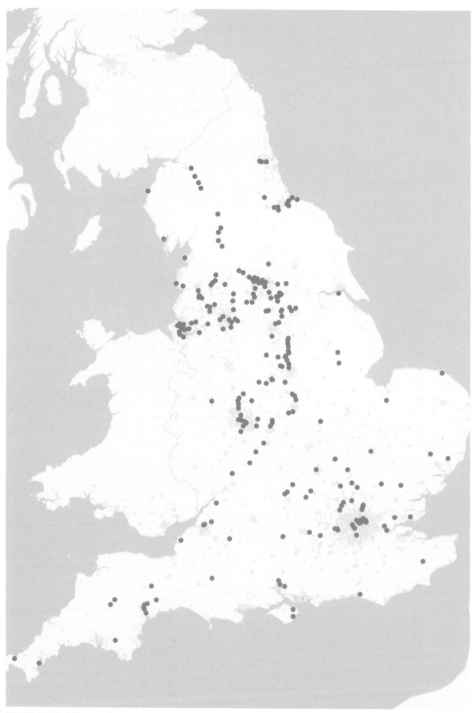

ENGLAND: Where the 251 new or reopened stations since 1960 are clustered

Chapter 1

How it was done

More than 400 stations and 950km of track have been added to the railway network since 1960. There has been no central government or rail industry plan to achieve this, but progress has come usually as a result of local or regional initiatives by rail managers, local authorities and rail campaigners. Some campaigns have been running for almost half a century, such as East West Rail.

There has been a significant and valuable input from the voluntary sector. Many reopenings or new facilities have resulted from Railfuture campaigns or local rail users' associations, as well as reopening campaigns affiliated to Railfuture. Sometimes this has taken the form of local fund-raising – such as at Watlington in 1975. Railfuture members also undertook sponsored cycle rides to raise money and publicise the case for reopening, including at Watton-at-Stone in 1982, when supporters were also encouraged to buy a brick at £3 each.

Public meetings were usually called, as at Arlesey, Bedfordshire, in 1985, where the high turn-out helped convince decision-makers of local demand. However, here and elsewhere it was also necessary to organise a survey of likely usage. In the case of Arlesey, we also had to find out which of three potential station sites was likely to attract the greatest number of passengers. The results helped persuade the local councils to put forward a funding package and the station opened in 1988.

In Wales, Railfuture campaigners have been very successful – with major triumphs such as the Vale of Glamorgan and Ebbw Valley reopenings. In 2009, the National Assembly for Wales commissioned studies for the reopening of freight lines from Aberdare to Hirwaun (Rhondda Cynon Taf) and Gaerwen to Llangefni (Sir Ynys Môn). Railfuture Wales made the case for these reopenings in *Wales the Rail Way Ahead,* which was first published in 1991.

In Staffordshire it took eight years to reopen the Cannock line, initially from Walsall as far as Hednesford, and again it was important for local campaigners to convince the county council that it should invest in the scheme. Public meetings were held, a local group was formed and several excursion trains were run as part of the campaign.

Excursion trains also played a significant part in Dereham, Norfolk. Railfuture and two local affiliated groups ran 20 passenger excursions over the freight-only line, aimed at both local people and visitors, from 1978 to 1988, after which British Rail closed it. The way forward for Dereham then had to be the formation of a preservation trust, the Mid-Norfolk Railway, which has progressively opened 25km of track to passenger traffic. The Wensleydale Railway in North Yorkshire, which Railfuture also supported, has been reopened in a similar manner. It is however still part of the national rail network, and aims to serve both local people and tourists. We first published a book, *Bring Back the Trains*, in 1983, with a second edition in 1984, advocating rail reopenings. From 1988 to 1998 we published four editions of the *A-Z of Rail Reopenings*, listing what had been achieved as well as pointing out potential new schemes. Many of the schemes we recommended in those publications have subsequently come to fruition.

Railfuture has held reopenings conferences, sometimes in towns such as Maesteg, Barry, Bathgate, Mansfield, Clitheroe, Corby, Stirling and Newtongrange where rail lines reopened. The conferences enabled delegates from many parts of the country to learn about how the reopenings were achieved and to pool their own experiences.

Sometimes in more recent years it has been necessary to engage with planning authorities in order to try to make potential reopenings easier. For example, in 2006 we and affiliated organisations objected to a planning application for a rowing lake at Willington, as it would cross the formation of the proposed East-West Rail Link and make rebuilding more expensive.

We also objected – unsuccessfully – to plans to convert the largely intact Cambridge to St Ives railway into a busway, arguing that it would be more sensible to reopen it as a railway for local, regional and national services. So campaigners have seen both heartache and success. The Government is poised in 2017 to embrace rail reopenings by cooperating with Railfuture and the Campaign for Better Transport in publishing *Expanding the Railway: how to develop and deliver a proposal.*

In 2010 we published *Britain's Growing Railway* to record progress and various stages of planning or construction. There were completely new lines and stations, as well as reopenings. We are pleased that, in 2017, it is necessary to update that book further.

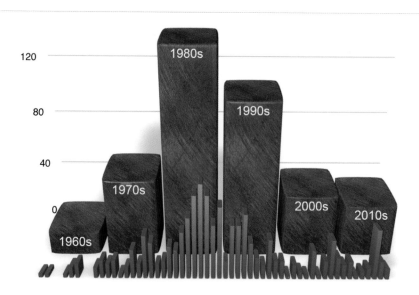

COUNTDOWN: This graph shows the number of stations reopened each year since 1960 (in blue) and the number opened in each decade (in brown)   Graph: Lloyd Butler

8

Chapter 2

From Abercynon to Ystrad

A-Z GUIDE TO NEW AND REOPENED STATIONS

More than 400 new and reopened stations on the national rail network as at July 2017 are catalogued here in A-Z order. The list relates to stations which have opened for services since 1960. For various reasons, a few have closed again, sometimes replaced by an even better facility nearby, or relocated a short distance away. Many of the new or reopened stations since 2000 are either in Scotland or South Wales, where the new national governments have taken a much more determined, pro-active and independent transport role. In England 250 stations have opened or reopened since 1960, compared to 100 in Scotland and 56 in Wales.

Some are out-of-town parkway stations or stations near airports. There is benefit in having passengers on the railways for part of their journey, but it also encourages car and air travel which competes with the railway, is less energy efficient and causes more pollution. Parkway stations can give some communities easier access to rail services.

ABERCYNON NORTH   03 Oct 1988
ABERCYNON GOGLEDD Rhondda Cynon Taf

Abercynon North station opened in 1988 along with five other stations on the former freight only line to Aberdare. Its opening led to the renaming of Abercynon's other station as Abercynon South. Since neither station met the Disability Discrimination Act, the Welsh Government merged the two stations, which were just 180 metres apart. In 2008 Abercynon North closed and investment was put into the South station which lost its suffix in the same year. An island platform was created and made DDA compliant. The station is now known simply as Abercynon and serves both the lines to Aberdare and Merthyr Tydfil.
Abercynon North annual passenger numbers: 275,404

ABERDARE   03 Oct 1988
ABERDÂR   Rhondda Cynon Taf

Opened on a site adjacent to the former Aberdare High Level station after a 34-year break, this four-car platform (two-car until 2005) is one of six along the Abercynon-

SCOTLAND: Where the 100 new or reopened stations since 1960 are clustered

Aberdare branch funded by the former Mid Glamorgan County Council.
Aberdare annual passenger numbers: 566,904

ADWICK South Yorkshire   11 Oct 1993

This two-platform station on the Doncaster-Leeds line cost £1 million and was funded
by South Yorkshire Passenger Transport Authority and Doncaster Council with a
contribution from the European Union.
Adwick annual passenger numbers: 205,618

AIGBURTH Merseyside   03 Jan 1978

Aigburth station (formerly Mersey Road and Aigburth) is on the southern section of
Liverpool's electric cross-city Northern line (Hunts Cross-Southport) service.
Aigburth annual passenger numbers: 833,452

AIRBLES North Lanarkshire   15 May 1989

Opened at a cost of £253,000 on the Hamilton Circle, this station serves the residential
area of south Hamilton, Motherwell College and Fir Park stadium, home of Motherwell
Football Club.
Airbles annual passenger numbers: 126,986

ALFRETON Derbyshire   07 May 1973

Alfreton and South Normanton station closed in 1967 but was reopened as a railhead
for passengers from the Mansfield area in 1973 and called Alfreton and Mansfield
Parkway. The station was renamed Alfreton in 1995 when a new Mansfield station was
opened near the town centre in Phase 2 of the Robin Hood line project.
Alfreton annual passenger numbers: 282,880

ALLENS WEST Stockton-on-Tees   04 Oct 1971

This station in the town of Eaglescliffe is on the Tees Valley line from Darlington to
Middlesbrough. The original station was opened in 1943, during the Second World War,
to serve an adjacent factory.
Allens West annual passenger numbers: 63,190

ALLOA Clackmannanshire   19 May 2008

This is the only new station on the Stirling-Alloa route, which was officially reopened to
passenger trains in 2008. Alloa has a population of 19,000, and is currently the terminus
for services from Glasgow Queen Street, although freight trains continue to Kincardine.
The new unstaffed station is on the site of the old Alloa Brewery and has a single bay
platform, a waiting room and train crew facilities. Transport Scotland said house prices
in Alloa started to rise more than a year before the station opened because people

WALES: Where the 56 new or reopened stations since 1960 are clustered

12

ALLOA: A train from Glasgow via Stirling arrives at Alloa station on 19 May 2008, the first day of public service on the reopened line. It proved extremely popular

wanted to live where they could catch a train. Once the route opened, there were more passengers than had been expected, about 8,000 per week. The conductor did not have time to sell tickets to all the passengers on board. A ticket machine, which had been thought unnecessary, had to be installed at the station to help cope with the demand.

Alloa annual passenger numbers: 386,528

ALNESS Ross and Cromarty   07 May 1973

Alness station, on the Far North line near Cromarty Firth, is 45km north of Inverness and 4.8km south of Invergordon. It reopened 13 years after being closed.

Alness annual passenger numbers: 23,614

ANDERSTON Glasgow   05 Nov 1979

Anderston station reopened 20 years after Anderston Cross station was closed. Its electric trains now serve the financial district of Glasgow. It was one of six new stations on the Argyle line reopened by British Rail and Strathclyde Passenger Transport Executive. The original building was demolished in 1968 to make way for the M8 motorway.

Anderston annual passenger numbers: 624,644

APPERLEY BRIDGE West Yorkshire   **13 Dec 2015**

Apperley Bridge on the electrified Leeds-Skipton line was West Yorkshire's first new rail station for 10 years. Funding problems delayed its opening for five years but within two years of opeing, it was hailed a runaway success. The new £10 million park-and-ride station has a 297-space car park and secure cycle parking. Its platforms are fully accessible, with staircases and ramps. The original station at Apperley Bridge closed in 1965. See also Kirkstall Forge which opened in June 2016.
Apperley Bridge annual passenger numbers: 96,418

ARDROSSAN TOWN North Ayrshire   **19 Jan 1987**

The station was closed in 1968 and was derelict for years. When the Ayrshire Coast line was electrified in the 1980s, it reopened with a single platform on the Harbour branch at a cost of £20,000.   Ardrossan Town annual passenger numbers: 20,068

ARGYLE STREET Glasgow   **05 Nov 1979**

Argyle Street station (formerly Glasgow Cross, closed 1964) was reopened as part of the Glasgow Central Low Level line reopening and electrification. It is now one of the busiest on the system.
Argyle Street annual passenger numbers: 1,382,948

ARLESEY Central Bedfordshire   **01 Oct 1988**

Closed on 5 January 1959, Arlesey station, on the East Coast main line between Hitchin and Biggleswade, was reopened at a cost of £630,000, with funding by county, district and parish councils. In 2012, the platforms were extended to accommodate 12-car trains, while a 400-space private car park on the west side of the station opened in 2014. As a result, between 2010 and 2015 footfall increased by over 50% to 627,000.
Arlesey annual passenger numbers: 667,602

ARMADALE West Lothian   **04 Mar 2011**

This station on the Airdrie-Bathgate line serves the 10,000 population of Armadale and includes parking for 200 cars. The station cleared the way for a £400 million regeneration project which has already delivered new homes and a supermarket. Future plans include more new homes, a multiplex cinema, a hotel, shops, cafes and restaurants, as well as business parks and extensive public parks.
See Chapter 4: New lines for passengers, Airdrie-Bathgate
Armadale annual passenger numbers: 215,390

ARMATHWAITE Cumbria   **14 Jul 1986**

Closed in May 1970, this Settle-Carlisle line station was reopened 16 years later with funding from Carlisle City, Eden District and Cumbria County councils.
Armathwaite annual passenger numbers: 5,950

ASHCHURCH FOR TEWKESBURY Gloucestershire **01 Jun 1997**

Closed in 1971, this £1 million station reopened with twin 97-metre platforms on the Bristol-Birmingham main line, serving Ashchurch and nearby Tewkesbury. Three train operators stop at the station, which was jointly funded by Gloucestershire County Council, Tewkesbury Borough Council and adjacent town and parish councils. Ashchurch for Tewkesbury annual passenger numbers: 91,000

ASHFIELD Glasgow **03 Dec 1993**

The new station at Ashfield was funded by Strathclyde Regional Council, and is on Glasgow's northern suburban line from Queen Street to Maryhill. Ashfield annual passenger numbers: 76,500

ASHFORD INTERNATIONAL Kent **08 Jan 1996**

A new name and new facilities were provided when Ashford station was rebuilt. Around £100 million was invested so the station could accommodate Eurostar trains on segregated platforms (3 and 4) with security screening and passport control areas, and domestic services on two new platforms (5 and 6). Despite Ashford having 600,000 international passengers in 2006, Railfuture was disappointed that when Ebbsfleet station opened, calls by Eurostar services at Ashford were cut by two-thirds, with only one train to and from Brussels restored in March 2009, none to Calais, and one to and from Lille. Campaigners have been fighting to persuade Eurostar to stop more trains at Ashford. From late 2009, Ashford International has also been served by domestic high-speed trains from London St Pancras. Ashford International annual passenger numbers: 3,764,590

AUCHINLECK East Ayrshire **12 May 1984**

This station, on the Dumfries-Kilmarnock line, closed in 1965 but reopened 19 years later at a cost of £218,000. There are trains to Glasgow, Carlisle and Newcastle but Stranraer passengers must change at Kilmarnock. Auchinleck annual passenger numbers: 61,986

AYLESBURY VALE PARKWAY Buckinghamshire **14 Dec 2008**

This £12 million single-platform station, near the A41 road, has a 500-space car park and was funded with £8.2 million from the Government's Community Infrastructure Fund, £1 million from Buckinghamshire County Council as part of a park-and-ride facility, £2.8 million from project manager Laing Rail, and 1.7 hectares of land from the developer of the Berryfields housing estate. Located north of Aylesbury, the reopening required the upgrading of almost 4km of freight-only line, doubling the line speed, plus signalling enhancements. It opened two years ahead of schedule in December 2008, without station buildings which were completed in June 2009. Served by extension of Chiltern Railways services from Marylebone every hour (half-hourly in peaks), it

is expected to form the first part of an extension of services to Milton Keynes via surviving freight lines, as part of the East West Rail project.
Aylesbury Vale Parkway annual passenger numbers: 168,610

B

BAGLAN Neath Port Talbot *Castell-nedd Port Talbot*   **02 Jun 1996**

This new station on the Swansea-Cardiff Swanline is west of Port Talbot and has twin 97-metre platforms with shelters, provided for £650,000. It is close to Neath Port Talbot general hospital.
Baglan annual passenger numbers: 26,882

BAILDON West Yorkshire   **05 Jan 1973**

Baildon, on the Shipley-Ilkley line, was closed in 1953, but reopened 20 years later with funds provided by Bradford City Council.
Baildon annual passenger numbers: 276,716

BAILLIESTON North Lanarkshire   **04 Oct 1993**

Glasgow's Baillieston station was closed in 1964 and then demolished, but the line remained open to freight. The new station was one of five that opened when passenger services were restored on the Glasgow Central to Whifflet line.
Baillieston annual passenger numbers: 126,234

BALMOSSIE Dundee   **18 Jun 1962**

A new station opened at Balmossie, 8km east of Dundee on the line to Aberdeen, in 1962 but after bus deregulation in 1985 it suffered from fierce bus competition at a time when trains were in short supply. The service was reduced in 1992, with only one train a day in each direction and none on Sundays.
Balmossie annual passenger numbers: 992

BARGEDDIE North Lanarkshire   **04 Oct 1993**

A new station opened at Bargeddie and four other locations when passenger trains were restored to the Glasgow Central to Whifflet line. The village's original station was closed in 1927.   Bargeddie annual passenger numbers: 95,214

BARROW-UPON-SOAR Leicestershire   **27 May 1994**

Barrow-upon-Soar and Quorn station closed in 1968 but a new twin-platform station on the Midland main line was reopened in 1994 by Transport Minister Roger Freeman,

to inaugurate the Ivanhoe line Phase 1 services between Loughborough and Leicester.
Barrow-upon-Soar annual passenger numbers: 631,364

BASILDON Essex   25 Nov 1974

This new twin-platform station, between Laindon and West Horndon on the London
Fenchurch Street to Southend line, serves the centre of the new town.
Basildon annual passenger numbers: 2,955,948

BATHGATE West Lothian   24 Mar 1986

This station reopened in 1986 and became the terminus for trains from Edinburgh
on the previously freight-only line from Edinburgh. The station was demolished in
2010 and rebuilt nearby as a two-platform through station as part of the Airdrie-
Bathgate line reopening. There were two months without trains but the new station is
adjacent to the town centre. For the 1986 reopening, there were track and signalling
improvements costing £380,000 and three new Sprinter trains costing £906,000.
The expense was shared by Lothian Regional Council, West Lothian District Council,
Scottish Development Agency, Livingston Development Corporation, and the
European Regional Development Fund. Passenger journeys of 264,000 per annum were
predicted, but by 1989 usage had already exceeded 1,000,000 passenger journeys per
annum.
See Chapter 4: New lines for passengers, Airdrie-Bathgate
Bathgate annual passenger numbers: 1,223,126

BEAULY Inverness   15 Apr 2002

The original Victorian station closed in 1960 but the station, with a platform long
enough for only one carriage, reopened on the Inverness-Dingwall line after much
wrangling about safety concerns. The £247,000 cost was jointly met by the Strategic
Rail Authority and local authorities. It is estimated that the reopening has led to 75%
of Beauly's commuters switching from road to rail. It has become the third most used
station north of Inverness.
Beauly annual passenger numbers: 59,406

BEDFORD ST JOHNS Bedford   14 May 1984

A new single-platform station on the Bedford-Bletchley line opened when services
from Bletchley were diverted into Bedford main station and the original Bedford
St Johns station was closed. Bedfordshire County Council contributed £40,000.
Bedford St Johns annual passenger numbers: 178,636

BEDWORTH Warwickshire   14 May 1988

The original Bedworth station closed and was demolished in 1965. After 23 years
without a station, Warwickshire County Council funded £50,000 of the £80,000 cost

of a new one. The station was initially served by a new Coventry-Nuneaton-Leicester service, but sadly this has now been reduced to a Coventry-Nuneaton shuttle. Bedworth annual passenger numbers: 83,086

BENTLEY South Yorkshire   27 Apr 1992

The £500,000 cost of this station was funded by South Yorkshire Passenger Transport Authority. It is served by hourly Doncaster-Leeds electric trains. Bentley annual passenger numbers: 140,724

BERMUDA PARK Warwickshire   18 Jan 2016

The £4.2 million station on the Nuneaton-Coventry line serves an industrial estate. Opening was delayed several times but, along with Coventry Arena, it eventually opened in January 2016. Bermuda Park is the first part of the NUCKLE plan to develop the route from Nuneaton to Coventry and Coventry to Leamington Spa, including a new platform at Coventry. The £13.6 million upgrade is being delivered by Coventry City Council, Centro and Warwickshire County Council with additional funding from the Department for Transport and the European Regional Development Fund. NUCKLE includes a new station at Kenilworth.
See Chapter 3: Stations opening soon, Kenilworth
Bermuda Park annual passenger numbers: 2,384

BERRY BROW West Yorkshire   09 Oct 1989

The original station closed in 1966. The reopened station on the Huddersfield-Penistone-Barnsley line was sponsored by West Yorkshire Passenger Transport Executive.
Berry Brow annual passenger numbers: 32,906

BICESTER VILLAGE Oxfordshire   26 Oct 2015

One-platform Bicester Town station closed in 2014 and reopened in 2015 as two-platform Bicester Village on Chiltern Railways' new route from London Marylebone to Oxford. Bicester Town station had been reopened in May 1987. The new station has a direct exit to Bicester Village shopping outlet which attracts six million shoppers a year, many of them from abroad. As trains arrive at the station, announcements are made in Japanese and Chinese. The town's population has grown from 17,500 in 1986 to 30,000. The Government has named Bicester as Britain's only garden town and has earmarked it for big housing developments. It anounced in 2014 that 13,000 homes would be built on the former Ministry of Defence depot. By 2036, Bicester is expected to have a population of 60,000.
See Chapter 4: New lines for passengers, Bicester-Oxford Parkway
Bicester Village annual passenger numbers: 413,432

BIRCHWOOD Cheshire   06 Oct 1980

This new station on the Manchester-Warrington-Liverpool line, with twin 208-metre platforms, a covered footbridge and a car park, was opened for £445,000, with £225,000 from British Rail, £160,000 from Warrington New Town and £60,000 from Cheshire County Council.
Birchwood annual passenger numbers: 670,450

BIRMINGHAM INTERNATIONAL West Midlands   26 Jan 1976

This major new station cost £5.9 million and was designed specifically to serve the National Exhibition Centre and the relocated Birmingham Airport terminal. The station on the West Coast main line has five 300-metre platforms and the vast car parking area attracts considerable park-and-ride traffic.
Birmingham International annual passenger numbers: 5,772,848

BIRMINGHAM MOOR STREET West Midlands   28 Sep 1987

New inter-city length twin platforms were opened on the new through lines alongside Moor Street terminal station, three platforms of which remained in use from 1972 to 1987. The original Grade II-listed Moor Street station has since been renovated at a cost of £11 million, and in 2010 Chiltern Railways connected two of the three terminal platforms to the network.
Birmingham Moor Street annual passenger numbers: 6,874,222

Picture: Philip Bisatt

BIRMINGHAM MOOR STREET: With the modern-day high-rise city in the background, a local train calls at the station, which has been able to retain its Great Western look

19

BIRMINGHAM MOOR STREET: Passengers like the traditional GWR look and feel

BIRMINGHAM SNOW HILL West Midlands   05 Oct 1987

This is a completely new four-platform station, built on the site of the former main line station which closed in 1972. The £8 million scheme was funded by the West Midlands Passenger Transport Executive, with a £900,000 European Regional Development Fund grant. This covered the construction of the new stations at Moor Street and Snow Hill, and the provision of new tracks and signalling. The station opened for local trains to Stratford-upon-Avon and Leamington Spa in 1987, and to the Smethwick line from September 1995. Snow Hill station also provides an interchange with the Midland Metro trams.

Birmingham Snow Hill annual passenger numbers: 4,713,174

BLACKPOOL PLEASURE BEACH Lancashire   13 Apr 1987

Blackpool Pleasure Beach station opened at a cost of £58,000, met by Blackpool Pleasure Beach Company (£31,000), British Rail (£15,000), Lancashire County Council (£10,000) and Blackpool Borough Council (£2,000).

Blackpool Pleasure Beach annual passenger numbers: 107,040

BLACKRIDGE West Lothian   12 Dec 2010
AN DRUIM DUBH

The station opened in 2010 on a new site, 600 metres closer to Edinburgh than the

previous Westcraigs station, as part of the Airdrie-Bathgate scheme. West Lothian Council backed the station reopening near the site of Westcraigs station which closed in 1956.
Blackridge annual passenger numbers: 53,194

BLAENAU FFESTINIOG Gwynedd   22 Mar 1982

The National Rail single-platform station has adjoining platforms for the private narrow-gauge Ffestiniog Railway. Closer to the town centre than the Blaenau Ffestiniog North station it replaced, it was opened by the House of Commons Speaker George Thomas. The FR operates primarily tourist passenger services to Porthmadog throughout most of the year. NR trains operate over the Conwy Valley line to Llandudno.
Blaenau Ffestiniog annual passenger numbers: 35,826

BLOXWICH West Midlands   17 Apr 1989

This two-platform station opened for Walsall-Hednesford trains on a former freight line at a new site north of the Bloxwich station that closed in 1965.
Bloxwich annual passenger numbers: 43,728

BLOXWICH NORTH West Midlands   02 Oct 1990

This two-platform station with timber-frame platforms, on the Chase line from Walsall to Hednesford, was opened at a cost of £280,000 to serve an area of new housing.
Bloxwich North annual passenger numbers: 46,730

BRAINTREE FREEPORT Essex   08 Sep 1999

Opened to provide public transport access to an extensive new leisure and retail development, this £1.1 million privately funded single-platform station is on the electrified Witham-Braintree branch line.
Braintree Freeport annual passenger numbers: 73,362

BRAMLEY West Yorkshire   12 Sep 1983

This station on the Bradford-Pudsey-Leeds Caldervale line, opened with timber platforms for £125,000, paid for by West Yorkshire Passenger Transport Executive. The original station closed in 1966.
Bramley annual passenger numbers: 317,342

BRANCHTON Inverclyde   05 Jun 1967

This new station on the Port Glasgow-Wemyss Bay line, effectively replaced the relocated former Greenock Upper Station.
Branchton annual passenger numbers: 121,696

BRIDGE OF ALLAN Stirling   13 May 1985

This station on the Stirling-Perth line reopened experimentally for £180,000, with
£120,000 from Central Regional Council and £60,000 from ScotRail. The original station
closed in 1965.
Bridge of Allan annual passenger numbers: 278,942

BRIDGETON Glasgow   05 Nov 1979

Part of the original Bridgeton Cross station, which closed in 1964, was reopened in 1979
when the Argyle line was created, a joint venture by British Rail and the Strathclyde
Passenger Transport Executive, reinstating many redundant sections of closed lines in
the Glasgow area. Five other stations on the Argyle line were also opened.
Bridgeton annual passenger numbers: 631,798

BRIGHOUSE West Yorkshire   28 May 2000

The original station, which had closed in 1970, reopened 30 years later with twin
97-metre platforms plus a CCTV-monitored 65-space car park to coincide with the
return of train services to the Huddersfield-Halifax Caldervale line.
Brighouse annual passenger numbers: 416,094

BRINNINGTON Greater Manchester   12 Dec 1977

This £240,000 new station in Stockport, on the Manchester Piccadilly-New Mills line,
was funded by Greater Manchester Passenger Transport Executive and has two
six-car platforms.
Brinnington annual passenger numbers: 78,548

BRISTOL PARKWAY South Gloucestershire   01 May 1972

This inter-city interchange and major parkway station opened following the
construction of nearby motorways and is at the intersection of two main rail lines to the
north of Bristol.
It became a three-platform station in 2007 when a new platform (called number 4!) was
opened along with other passenger facilities such as a new booking hall and customer
help desk in a £3.3 million scheme. This followed £4 million worth of enhancements in
2001 that included a new footbridge and lifts.
Bristol Parkway annual passenger numbers: 2,511,016

BRITISH STEEL REDCAR Redcar and Cleveland   19 Jun 1978

This new station was opened on the Middlesbrough-Saltburn Tees Valley line to serve
the steel works. There is no public access to the station.
British Steel (Redcar) annual passenger numbers: 740

BRITON FERRY Neath Port Talbot

01 Jun 1994

LLANSAWEL Castell-nedd Port Talbot

The twin 108-metre platform station with ramp access is located between Neath and Port Talbot for the Swanline services linking Swansea and Cardiff.
Briton Ferry annual passenger numbers: 35,224

BROMBOROUGH RAKE Merseyside

30 Sep 1985

On the newly electrified Hooton line into the Wirral, this new station cost £200,000 which was met by Merseyside Passenger Transport Executive with a European Regional Development Fund grant.
Bromborough Rake annual passenger numbers: 298,204

BRUNSTANE Edinburgh

03 Jun 2002

Situated on a reopened freight line south of Portobello, this new 143-metre single platform opened to Crossrail services, operating from Edinburgh Park to Newcraighall. Network Rail has proposed doubling the track to increase capacity. If this happens, a second platform will be built.
Brunstane annual passenger numbers: 165,978

BRUNSWICK Merseyside

09 Mar 1998

Located in Dingle, Brunswick station is south of Liverpool Central station on Merseyrail's Northern line, between Central and St Michael's stations. The £2.9 million cost was met with contributions of £1.6 million from Merseytravel, £1 million of European funding, £325,000 from Merseyside Development Corporation, and urban regeneration grant funding.
Brunswick annual passenger numbers: 929,958

BUCKSHAW PARKWAY Lancashire

03 Oct 2011

Lancashire County Council co-ordinated the project to construct £6.8 million Buckshaw Parkway station, between Chorley and Preston. Planning permission was granted in August 2008, several months before the Government announced the line was to be electrified. Network Rail applied to build the station to serve 2,000 new homes on the former Royal Ordnance factory site at Euxton. Work was part-funded through a 'Section 106' agreement. Lancashire County Council contributed £3.3 million. The station consists of a modular two-floor building, with booking hall, ticket office, store, staff facilities and toilets on the ground floor, with plant rooms above, two 150-metre single-face platforms (with potential to extend by 60 metres) each with a canopy, and a single-span pedestrian access bridge over the railway line with lifts at either end. There is parking for 204 cars and 50 cycles.
Buckshaw Parkway annual passenger numbers: 303,892

BULWELL Nottinghamshire 27 May 1994

This station was built subsequent to the start of Phase 1 services on the Nottingham-Worksop Robin Hood line. The cost of £900,000 was met by Nottingham City Council. Trams stop next to the station.
Bulwell annual passenger numbers: 57,716

BURLEY PARK West Yorkshire 29 Nov 1988

This new station was built on the line from Leeds to Harrogate and is very popular with commuters into Leeds.
Burley Park annual passenger numbers: 697,856

BURNLEY MANCHESTER ROAD Lancashire 29 Sep 1986

This station, sited adjacent to the previous one which closed in 1961, was reopened experimentally to serve the Copy Pit line. The cost of £139,000 was largely met by £127,000 from the county council. With the 2014/15 £8.8 million reinstatement of the Todmorden south-to-west curve, which allowed trains to run between Burnley and Manchester via Rochdale in less than an hour for the first time in 40 years, the station was upgraded at a cost of £2.3 million.
Burnley Manchester Road annual passenger numbers: 393,304

CALDERCRUIX North Lanarkshire 13 Feb 2011

This two-platform station serves the 5,000 population of Caldercruix, on the Airdrie-Bathgate line.
See Chapter 4: New lines for passengers, Airdrie-Bathgate.
Caldercruix annual passenger numbers: 111,472

CAM & DURSLEY Gloucestershire 29 May 1994

This new twin-platform station on the Bristol-Birmingham main line between Gloucester and Yate cost £500,000 and was funded by Gloucestershire County Council with contributions from other local councils. A ramp footbridge, car park and bus link have been provided.
Cam & Dursley annual passenger numbers: 193,640

CAMBRIDGE NORTH: Nearing completion in March 2017

CAMBRIDGE NORTH Cambridgeshire   21 May 2017

The £50 million station at Chesterton junction serves the Science Park and includes three platforms for 12-coach trains, as well as parking for 1,000 bicycles and 450 cars. Its distinctive silver cladding is based on the computer model Game of Life, created by mathematician John Conway when he was a lecturer at Cambridge University. Solar panels should provide 10% of its power needs. Access links to the site for the guided bus were built by Cambridgeshire County Council. The new station is served by King's Cross fast and stopping and Liverpool Street stopping trains plus regular Ely and Norwich services. Council leader Steve Count commented: "Cambridge North station will be a real asset to the city and the wider area in both boosting the local economy and giving local people greater transport options." The station was funded by the Department for Transport and developed by Network Rail in partnership with the county council. The 2018 Thameslink service to Brighton will start from Cambridge North, and from 2019 the Norwich-Stansted Airport service will also call. After the successful opening of Cambridge North, thoughts are already turning to whether a third station could be on its way for the south of the city. Discussions over a possible station at Addenbrooke's Hospital, to be called either Cambridge South or Addenbrooke's, are under way.

CAMELON Falkirk   27 Sep 1994

This station on the Falkirk-Glasgow and Edinburgh-Stirling routes was opened at a cost of £1.1 million funded by Central Regional Council. This was ScotRail's 50th new station in 10 years and has attracted a healthy level of patronage from the start. Camelon annual passenger numbers: 136,100

CANNOCK Staffordshire   08 Apr 1989

Reinstatement of platforms provided one of the five new stations funded by
Staffordshire County Council and West Midlands Passenger Transport Executive on the
Walsall-Hednesford line. The original station had closed in 1965.
Cannock annual passenger numbers: 220,290

CARMYLE Glasgow   04 Oct 1993

This is one of five stations reopened with Strathclyde Regional Council funding when
the freight-only Glasgow-Whifflet line was restored for passenger use.
Carmyle annual passenger numbers: 132,454

CATHAYS Cardiff *Caerdydd*   03 Oct 1983

This £83,000 station was opened to serve the office and university area of North Cardiff.
The cost was met by £80,000 from South Glamorgan County Council and £3,000 from
Mid Glamorgan County Council. When opened, 600 passenger journeys per day were
expected, but the five-year target was reached within the first three months! It is
within a short walk of the Welsh Assembly buildings. The two platforms were recently
extended to accommodate six-car trains. Cathays annual passenger numbers: 903,646

CHAFFORD HUNDRED Essex   30 May 1995

With a 12-car platform, this new station opened to serve a housing development and
the massive Lakeside shopping centre alongside the Upminster-Grays line. The station
proved so popular with both commuters and leisure travellers that the original small
ticket office and limited circulating area were no longer adequate. In September 2006,
Rail Minister Derek Twigg opened a brand new booking office and waiting area. The
forecourt was also completely redesigned and landscaped by Thurrock Council.
Chafford Hundred annual passenger numbers: 2,534,474

CHANDLER'S FORD Hampshire   19 Oct 2003

A new single platform opened here, on the freight-only single-track route, to serve
a new hourly cross-rail service for South Hampshire linking Romsey, Eastleigh,
Southampton and Totton. The £2 million capital cost of the platform, station premises,
50-space car park, cycle link, CCTV and land purchase was funded by a £1.4 million
Local Transport Plan grant and a £600,000 developer contribution. The original 1847
station had closed in 1969.   Chandler's Ford annual passenger numbers: 224,034

CHATELHERAULT South Lanarkshire   12 Dec 2005

One of two new intermediate single-platform stations on the reopened line to Larkhall,
now served by electric trains from Glasgow.
Chatelherault annual passenger numbers: 85,898

CHANDLER'S FORD: Balloons go up in 2003 as passengers flock to the new station

CITY THAMESLINK Greater London   29 May 1990

This station near Ludgate Circus replaced the Holborn Viaduct terminus which closed in 1990. Its new low-level alignment allowed the later demolition of the rail bridge over Ludgate Hill. The station was opened as St Paul's Thameslink but was renamed in 1991 to avoid confusion with St Paul's Central line Tube station. It was built with 12-car platforms ready for the Thameslink 2000 project. In 2009 the station was given a £4.5 million facelift.   City Thameslink annual passenger numbers: 6,340,256

CLITHEROE Lancashire   08 Apr 1987

This station reopened having been renovated at a cost of £2,800 to enable monthly summertime Dalesrail trains to call. The costs were contributed to by Lancashire County Council, the Countryside Commission, Ribble Valley District Council, and Clitheroe Town Council. From May 1990 the platform was used for a Saturdays-only service of four trains each way. From May 1994 regular trains have called at this and three other newly built stations on this line.
Clitheroe annual passenger numbers: 240,112

Picture: Three Rivers Community Rail Partnership

COLESHILL PARKWAY Warwickshire   19 Aug 2007

In March 2006 the Secretary of State for Transport agreed to contribute £4.1 million towards the £8.3 million cost of building this new station in North Warwickshire between Water Orton and Nuneaton on the Birmingham-Derby main line. This scheme was the UK railway's first part Public-Private Partnership and part Private Finance Initiative. Warwickshire County Council, which contributed £2 million, had planned a station for several years and was supported by Network Rail in its draft route utilisation strategy for the West Midlands. Laing Rail Projects, which contributed the remaining £2 million in return for a share of the revenue earned for the two trains per hour, managed the development. It sub-contracted the building work to Carillion. This fully staffed station consists of two 75-metre platforms, a 200-space car park and four bus bays. The previous station, named Forge Mills until 1923, closed in 1968.
Coleshill Parkway annual passenger numbers: 266,654

CONON BRIDGE Ross-shire (Highland Region)   08 Feb 2013

Famous, or notorious, for having a platform only 15 metres long, a new £600,000 station opened at Conon Bridge, after the previous station closed in 1960. The station, between Dingwall and Inverness, provided an alternative to driving during the £18 million repairs to Kessock Bridge on the A9 road. Highland Council contributed £100,000 towards the costs of reopening and a further £100,000 to upgrade the car park. The new station was forecast to handle 36,000 passengers a year, including tourists and commuters to Inverness. It is lit by environmentally friendly LEDs and the shelter lighting is provided by solar panels on the roof.
Conon Bridge annual passenger numbers: 15,276

CONONLEY North Yorkshire   21 Apr 1988

This station on the Skipton-Keighley line reopened with contributions from the Rural Development Commission, North Yorkshire County Council, district and parish councils, towards the £34,000 cost. By September 1989, the daily passenger journeys of 135 were double that required to justify its reopening.
Cononley annual passenger numbers: 168,366

CONWAY PARK Merseyside   22 Jun 1998

This new underground station on the New Brighton and West Kirby lines, north of Birkenhead town centre, is an integral part of a seven-hectare development. Extensive deep construction work and good access requirements incurred a substantial £15.7 million cost, which was shared by the local transport authority Merseytravel, Wirral Council, City Challenge funding and European grants. It is provided with twin 130-metre platforms, escalators, lifts, emergency stairs and a surface ticket hall.
Conway Park annual passenger numbers: 1,061,164

CONWY Conwy   27 Jun 1987

Located within the mediaeval walled town of Conwy, this £267,000 station on the

Holyhead main line reopened as an experiment. The twin platforms are of two-car length. The trains are often three-cars long but only one door opens at Conwy. This causes problems when passengers, some carrying luggage, bicycles or prams, have to board and alight through the same door. The summer Saturday locomotive-hauled holiday extra trains cannot call at Conwy because of the short platforms. Conwy is a request stop which foreign visitors are often confused by. The station was funded by Gwynedd County Council and the Welsh Office.
Conwy annual passenger numbers: 46,336

CORBY Northamptonshire　　　13 Apr 1987　　23 Feb 2009

A new station opened in 2009, 22 years after an earlier reopening failed. The station, which is adjacent to the site of the old station, provides parking for around 140 cars, and has a taxi rank and bus interchange. Construction of the station, made from prefabricated components assembled on site, started in July 2008. Opening was delayed because of a lack of rolling stock. In 2017, preparatory work was under way to clear the ground for electrification masts. Since the 1960s Corby had been on a freight-only branch which saw occasional passenger service diversions. An experimental Corby-Kettering shuttle service began in 1987 and ended in June 1990. The shuttle suffered from having an irregular timetable, with no peak-hour services to connect with trains to and from London, and the use of unreliable 30-year-old diesel trains.

Picture: Elisabeth Jordan

CORBY: It's early in the morning on 23 February 2009 and passengers prepare to welcome trains back to Corby, 22 years after an earlier unsuccessful reopening

Northamptonshire County Council paid a fixed fee for the service and took the entire ticket revenue. No railcard discounts or through ticketing were available. Patronage did not cover operating costs and the council was unwilling to assist with funding. After the shuttle service ceased, there was considerable business pressure for a reopened railway station and the Department for Transport asked bidders for the East Midlands franchise (which started in November 2007) to price the cost of extending the hourly London-Kettering service to Corby.

In August 2007, a planning application was submitted by North Northantonshire Development Company and English Partnerships to build the new £10.22 million station at Corby. Other partners included East Midlands Development Agency. For the longer term, Railfuture is lobbying for a regular northbound service from Corby. Corby annual passenger numbers: 278,198

CORKERHILL Glasgow   30 Jul 1990

Costing £120,000, this was one of the five new stations funded by Strathclyde Regional Council on the freight-only Paisley Canal line in South Glasgow opened experimentally to electric services. Corkerhill annual passenger numbers: 266,154

COTTINGLEY West Yorkshire   25 Apr 1988

This new station is on the Leeds-Dewsbury line. It was opened by British Rail with financial assistance from West Yorkshire Passenger Transport Executive. Cottingley annual passenger numbers: 88,810

COVENTRY ARENA Warwickshire   18 January 2016

The £3.4 million new station on the Nuneaton-Coventry line serves an industrial estate and is supposed to serve the sports arena. Opening was delayed several times and attracted adverse publicity at first when a shortage of trains meant that it could not be used on Coventry City football or Wasps rugby match days, although train operator London Midland hired charter trains on some Wasp match days because the normal one-coach service was completely inadequate. Some commentators said the money spent on the station was a waste but in the long-term it may prove a success for match days as well as with commuters.
See also Bermuda Park.
Coventry Arena annual passenger numbers: 11, 964

CRANBROOK Devon   13 Dec 2015

Cranbrook was the second new station in Devon to open in 2015 (see Newcourt) and two more are planned – at Marsh Barton and Edginswell. The £5 million Cranbrook station is spacious with a 150-space car park, bus interchange and safe walking route to the new "eco community" near Exeter airport. There are through trains to London Waterloo and the journey to Exeter Central is under 10 minutes, compared to at least 30 minutes by bus. Cranbrook is part of the county council's Devon Metro plan to create an alternative to car use. The station can handle six-car trains.
Cranbrook annual passenger numbers: 20,404

COVENTRY ARENA: A new station, but a better train service is needed

CRESSINGTON Merseyside   03 Jan 1978

This very attractive Grade II-listed reopened station is on Merseyrail's Northern line. The station had previously closed in 1972.
Cressington annual passenger numbers: 476,636

CRESWELL Derbyshire   24 May 1998

Creswell opened along with three other stations during Phase 3 of the Robin Hood line extension from Mansfield to Worksop. The station has standard twin 79-metre platforms and cost approximately £600,000.
Creswell annual passenger numbers: 40,766

CROOKSTON Glasgow   30 Jul 1990

One of the five new stations on the Paisley Canal line, this station was opened at a cost of £105,000.
Crookston annual passenger numbers: 174,822

CROSSFLATTS West Yorkshire   17 May 1982

This timber twin-platform station was newly opened to serve the Airedale line (Leeds to Keighley and Skipton) at a cost of £78,000.
Crossflatts annual passenger numbers: 524,846

CROSSKEYS Caerphilly *Caerffili*   07 Jun 2008

This two-platform station was the sixth to be opened on the Ebbw Valley line, four months after the line reopened to passengers. The station is at the end of the double track passing loop between Risca and Crosskeys. Leaving Crosskeys, trains enter the single track which extends to the railhead at Ebbw Vale Parkway.
Cross Keys annual passenger numbers: 118,742

CURRIEHILL Edinburgh   05 Oct 1987

This is an experimentally reopened station 11km from Edinburgh on the line to Glasgow via Shotts. The £273,000 cost was met by Lothian Regional Council.
Curriehill annual passenger numbers: 67,020

CWMBACH Rhondda Cynon Taf   03 Oct 1988

A single two-car platform station was reopened on the Abercynon-Aberdare line and subsequently extended to take four-car trains.
Cwmbach annual passenger numbers: 24,606

CWMBRAN Torfaen   12 May 1986

This station opened between Newport and Pontypool, at a cost of £215,000 partly met by Cwmbrân Development Corporation, which contributed £165,000 and also provided a 160-space car park. The station has twin 122-metre platforms, a footbridge, waiting rooms and ticket office. A new booking office and improved station facilities were opened in 2009.
Cwmbran annual passenger numbers: 375,614

DALGETY BAY Fife   28 Mar 1998

Located on the Fife Circle between Inverkeithing and Aberdour, just north of Inverkeithing, this £1.5 million station was funded by contributions from a local developer and Fife Regional Council. It has twin four-car length platforms, a ramped footbridge and an 83-space car park.
Dalgety Bay annual passenger numbers: 340,972

DALMARNOCK Glasgow   05 Nov 1979

This station was reopened as part of the reinstatement of the Argyle line and was one of six new stations opened on this line. Being close to the Commonwealth Arena and Sir Chris Hoy Velodrome, it benefited from more than £2.8 million of European Regional Development Fund prior to the Commonwealth Games in Glasgow in 2014.
Dalmarnock annual passenger numbers: 283,204

DALSTON JUNCTION Greater London   27 Apr 2010

The original 1865 North London Railway station closed in 1986 when the line from Broad Street station closed. The 2010 reopened station is part of London Overground's East London line. The completely rebuilt station has two platform islands, with westbound services going to Highbury and Islington. Hopes of reopening the eastbound curve have faded since 2010.
See Chapter 4: New lines for passengers, East London line
Dalston Junction annual passenger numbers: 5,139,640

DALSTON KINGSLAND Greater London   17 May 1983

This new station, on the North London line, opened at a cost of £650,000 which was met by the Greater London Council and an Urban Programme Grant. The station is on the site of the original Kingsland station which closed in 1865 when Dalston Junction station opened. The street level building, however, survived for well over 100 years.
Dalston Kingsland annual passenger numbers: 5,931,382

DANESCOURT Cardiff *Caerdydd*   04 Oct 1987

On the former freight-only City line immediately west of Cardiff, Danescourt is one of four stations on this 8km route funded by former South Glamorgan County Council.
Danescourt annual passenger numbers: 104,278

DEIGHTON West Yorkshire   26 Apr 1982

Just north of Huddersfield, and on the site of a station closed in 1930, the new Deighton station opened at a cost of £65,000 – met by West Yorkshire Passenger Transport Authority.
Deighton annual passenger numbers: 95,648

DENT Cumbria   14 Jul 1986

Reopened for the Dalesrail services over the Settle and Carlisle line, this station received funding from Cumbria County Council. Dent is famous as the highest railway station in England.
Dent annual passenger numbers: 8,484

DERKER Greater Manchester   30 Aug 1985

This station opened experimentally and is 1km north of Oldham Mumps station. Both the station and the Oldham loop line closed in 2009 for three years, to allow them to be included in the Manchester light-rail Metrolink system. Derker became a tram stop on the Oldham and Rochdale line of Metrolink in 2012.

DIGBY & SOWTON Devon   23 May 1995

The single 108-metre platform is 5km south of Exeter Central on the Exmouth line. The £700,000 station has an access ramp, shelter and a 500-space car park for both rail and bus park-and-ride services. A nearby Tesco supermarket contributed £200,000 towards the station, with the balance coming from Devon County Council. The station became the busiest unstaffed station in the West Country.
Digby & Sowton annual passenger numbers: 561,188

DODWORTH South Yorkshire   16 May 1989

Opened on the Penistone to Barnsley line, 5km from Barnsley, this station replaced one that closed in 1959.   Dodworth annual passenger numbers: 47,944

DOLGARROG Conwy   14 Jun 1965

Dolgarrog station reopened on the Conwy Valley line from Blaenau Ffestiniog to Llandudno in 1965. An earlier station closed the year before.
Dolgarrog annual passenger numbers: 1,474

DRONFIELD Derbyshire   05 Jan 1981

Midway between Chesterfield and Sheffield, this station was reopened at a cost of £90,000 funded by Derbyshire County Council, who found £60,000, and the North East Derbyshire District Council. The original station closed in 1967 and the buildings were demolished.
Dronfield annual passenger numbers: 199,868

DRUMFROCHAR Inverclyde   24 May 1998

A modest single 123-metre platform opened in the south-west part of Greenock. It cost £750,000 and was funded by Strathclyde Passenger Transport Authority. Drumfrochar is served by Glasgow to Wemyss Bay trains.
Drumfrochar annual passenger numbers: 68,438

DRUMGELLOCH North Lanarkshire   06 Mar 2011

Drumgelloch station is on the reopened Airdrie-Bathgate rail line which opened up a fourth rail link between Glasgow and Edinburgh. The station has a 336-space car park

Picture: Philip Bisatt

DUMBRECK: This £298,000 station on the former freight-only Paisley Canal line reopened in 1990 on the site of Bellahouston station, which closed in 1954

including 18 spaces for less able travellers, and a dedicated area for cyclists. The station did not open for passenger traffic when the line opened on 12 December 2010 and passengers wishing to start or complete their journey at Drumgelloch initially had to transfer to a replacement bus service at Airdrie. The station finally reopened on 6 March 2011. An earlier single-platform station was opened in May 1989 as the terminus of a 2.5km extension from Airdrie on the Glasgow North electric line. An earlier station called Clarkston closed in 1956.
See Chapter 4: New Lines for Passengers, Airdrie-Bathgate
Drumgelloch annual passenger numbers: 403,546

DUMBRECK Glasgow   30 Jul 1990

Reopened on the site of the original Bellahouston station (closed in 1954), this two-platform station cost £298,000, funded by Strathclyde Regional Council, one of five new stations on the former freight-only Paisley Canal line.
Dumbreck annual passenger numbers: 164,044

DUNCRAIG Wester Ross   03 May 1976

This remote station – built to serve a castle on the shores of Loch Carron near Kyle of Lochalsh – was reopened 12 years after it lost its train service.
Duncraig annual passenger numbers: 494

DYCE: A train from Inverness, left, and a train from Aberdeen in June 2014

DUNFERMLINE QUEEN MARGARET Fife   26 Jan 2000

Just east of Dunfermline Town station, this £1.8 million station has twin 110-metre platforms, a ramped footbridge and a 93-space car park. Fully funded by Fife Council, the station serves Queen Margaret Hospital (which opened 15 years earlier) and a housing development.
Dunfermline Queen Margaret annual passenger numbers: 250,538

DUNLOP East Ayrshire   05 Jun 1967

This station is on the Glasgow-Kilmarnock line and reopened a year after being closed. There was an angry public reaction to the closure and a press campaign in favour of reopening. A second platform was added in 2008. Services were doubled in December 2009 – to a train every half hour – after another successful local campaign.
Dunlop annual passenger numbers: 95,498

DUNROBIN CASTLE Sutherland   30 Jun 1985

Originally a private station on the Far North line for the Duke of Sutherland's castle home, Dunrobin Castle was reopened, initially on a summer-only request stop basis. It had closed 20 years earlier.
Dunrobin Castle annual passenger numbers: 782

36

DUNSTON Tyne and Wear · 01 Oct 1984

This Newcastle-Carlisle line station was opened at a cost of £90,000, shared between British Rail and Gateshead District Council, after services were re-routed following the closure of Scotswood Bridge. It now retains only an infrequent service.
Dunston annual passenger numbers: 7,168

DYCE Aberdeen · 15 Sep 1984

Dyce station reopened experimentally to serve the airport and commuters to Aberdeen after it was closed in 1968. The £3,500 cost was met by Grampian Regional Council. Patronage was four times higher than predicted within a year of it opening. Some 75,000 passenger journeys per annum were initially expected but patronage had reached 340,000 by 1985.
Dyce annual passenger numbers: 664,396

EAST GARFORTH West Yorkshire · 01 May 1987

A new station on the Leeds-York line was provided at a cost of £110,000 met by West Yorkshire Passenger Transport Executive. By 1988, the expected 200 passenger journeys per day had quadrupled.
East Garforth annual passenger numbers: 238,614

EAST MIDLANDS PARKWAY Nottinghamshire · 26 Jan 2009

The latest environmental techniques, including ground water heating and grey water recycling, making use of locally sourced and recycled materials, were used in this station. Outline planning permission was given in 2001 for the £25.5 million four-platform 850-space parkway station next to the M1 motorway at Ratcliffe-on-Soar. A shuttle bus serves nearby East Midlands Airport but long-distance road coaches also serve the station. Construction was held up by E.ON, which owned land needed for access roads, but began in December 2007. Mainly funded by Network Rail, £895,000 was contributed by East Midlands Development Agency.
East Midlands Parkway annual passenger numbers: 306,408

EASTBROOK Vale of Glamorgan *Bro Morgannwg* · 24 Nov 1986

This station near Dinas Powys on the Barry line has shelters and a footbridge, serving two platforms. The station, with car parking, cost £106,000 – shared between British Rail and South Glamorgan County Council.
Eastbrook annual passenger numbers: 176,506

EASTHAM RAKE Wirral, Merseyside   03 Apr 1995

Built at a cost of £2 million and funded by Merseyside Passenger Transport Executive, this new station on the Liverpool Central to Chester line is served by electric trains on the Merseyrail DC network.
Eastham Rake annual passenger numbers: 328,052

EBBSFLEET INTERNATIONAL Kent   19 Nov 2007

This new £180 million station on High Speed 1 (formerly known as the Channel Tunnel Rail Link) is between Stratford (east London) and Ashford International. It opened five days after St Pancras International. Ebbsfleet has two platforms for daily Eurostar services to Paris and Brussels (change trains at Lille), and four platforms for the domestic Javelin commuter trains which started running in 2009.
With a notional catchment area of 10 million people, Ebbsfleet has 9,000 car park spaces with 3,000 spaces available for domestic passengers. Planning consent has been given for offices, shops, and homes nearby. However, there is no interchange with other domestic services on the North Kent line to/from Dartford and south-east London stations, nor any pedestrian access to Northfleet station, only 600 metres away.
Ebbsfleet International annual passenger numbers: 1,673,686

Picture: Bruce Williamson

EBBW VALE PARKWAY: This was the new terminus station for the line which reopened in February 2008. The terminus is now Ebbw Vale Town

EBBW VALE PARKWAY   Blaenau Gwent   06 Feb 2008
PARCFFORDD GLYN EBWY

This new single-platform station adjacent to the site of the former Victoria station was the terminus on the Ebbw Valley line for seven years. Its reopening was welcomed by one developer, who offered a year's free rail travel to Cardiff for anyone reserving a new home at its nearby Cae Ffwrnais estate. The Welsh Government expected the trains to carry their millionth passenger after four years but that milestone was passed in just 20 months. Based on those incorrect estimates of use, and to save money, only 5km of double track was provided.
See Chapter 4: New lines for passengers, Ebbw Valley line
Ebbw Vale Parkway annual passenger numbers: 101,634

EBBW VALE TOWN Blaenau Gwent   17 May 2015
TREF GLYN EBWY

Ebbw Vale Town station, on the site of the former Corus steelworks, opened seven years after the line from Cardiff was reopened and was funded by the Welsh Government. New track was needed to extend the line by 2.5km from Ebbw Vale Parkway. The new station can accommodate a six-car train and an inclined lift links the station to the town.
See Chapter 4: New lines for passengers, Ebbw Valley line
Ebbw Vale Town annual passenger numbers: 167,642

EDINBURGH GATEWAY Edinburgh   11 Dec 2016

The newest addition to Scotland's railway map, Edinburgh Gateway, was opened by Transport Minister Humza Yousaf. The £41 million tram-train interchange on the western side of the city is designed to provide easy access to the airport and the tram network, particularly for rail travellers from Perth, Dundee, Inverness and Fife. The interchange will allow rail passengers to complete their journey to the terminal building by tram. The station was funded as part of EGIP (Edinburgh Glasgow Improvement Programme). The platforms can accommodate 10-car trains. The station is between South Gyle and Dalmeny on the Fife Circle line and is served by improved Edinburgh-Fife rail services. It was built next to the Gogar roundabout on the A8 road. The station is expected to be a catalyst for future economic investment.

EDINBURGH PARK Edinburgh   04 Dec 2003

Close to the business park in South Gyle and Hermiston Gate shopping centre, this new two-platform station is served by trains from Edinburgh to Glasgow via Bathgate, and to Dunblane via Stirling. A tram provides onward connections to Edinburgh Airport. The overall investment of £5 million was funded by £1.5 million each from the City of Edinburgh Council and New Edinburgh Ltd, and £1.9 million from the Strategic Rail Authority's rail passenger partnership fund. The station was also supported by the Scottish Executive and ScotRail. Initial predictions had suggested only 500 daily passengers, but by 2005 the station was actually handling 1,100 passengers daily. Edinburgh Park annual passenger numbers: 889,460

ENERGLYN & CHURCHILL PARK Caerphilly   16 Dec 2013
ENEU'R-GLYN A PHARC CHURCHILL Caerffili

Trains began using the £5 million Energlyn & Churchill Park railway station on 8 December 2013 before it was formally opened by Edwina Hart, the Welsh Government Transport Minister. The northbound platform is in the Energlyn suburb of Caerphilly, while the southbound one is in Churchill Park. The station is between Llanbradach and Aber. It was developed by the Welsh Government, Network Rail, Caerphilly County Borough Council, the South East Wales Transport Alliance and Arriva Trains Wales.
Energlyn & Churchill Park annual passenger numbers: 74,206

ESKBANK Midlothian   6 Sep 2015

Eskbank station was one of seven new stations on the reopened Borders Railway from Edinburgh Waverley to Tweedbank. Single-platform Eskbank is a few hundred metres from the earlier station site and is close to Bonnyrigg and Dalkeith. It provides access to the community hospital and is a 10-minute rail link between Edinburgh College and its Midlothian campus.
See Chapter 4: New lines for passengers, Edinburgh-Tweedbank
Eskbank annual passenger numbers: 128,298

EUXTON BALSHAW LANE Lancashire   15 Dec 1997

The £1 million station served by Wigan-Preston trains, opened initially on a five-year experimental basis. New twin 108-metre platforms were built on the slow lines of the West Coast main line, south of Leyland and Euxton junction.
Euxton Balshaw Lane annual passenger numbers: 72,726

EXHIBITION CENTRE Glasgow   05 Nov 1979

This station serves the Scottish Exhibition and Conference Centre and is between Anderston and Partick. It was one of six new stations opened when the Argyle line was restored. Exhibition Centre was initially called Finnieston but renamed 10 years later. The original Stobcross station closed in 1959.
Exhibition Centre annual passenger numbers: 1,742,528

FAIRWATER   Cardiff   04 Oct 1987
Y TYLLGOED   *Caerdydd*

One of four new stations on the Cardiff City line, it was funded by the former South Glamorgan County Council.   Fairwater annual passenger numbers: 70,910

FALLS OF CRUACHAN   Argyll and Bute   20 Jun 1988

Located at the foot of Ben Cruachan, on the Oban branch of the West Highland line, this station reopened with a £10,000 platform to serve the underground hydro-electric power station. British Rail achieved the low cost by constructing the platform using redundant concrete sleepers and topping it with slabs. There is also a visitor centre and tours through the access tunnels. The original station had closed in 1965.
Falls of Cruachan annual passenger numbers: 734

FALMOUTH TOWN   Cornwall   07 Dec 1970

This was opened as Falmouth, a new terminus when BR cut back the line in 1970. It was renamed Falmouth (The Dell) in 1975 when the station at the docks reopened as Falmouth Docks. Falmouth (The Dell) was re-named Falmouth Town in 1989.
Falmouth Town annual passenger numbers: 203,468

FEATHERSTONE   West Yorkshire   11 May 1992

Opened on the former freight-only Wakefield to Pontefract line, 10km east of Wakefield Kirkgate station, this station replaced a previous one which had closed in 1967.
Featherstone annual passenger numbers: 66,024

FENITON   Devon   03 May 1971

A modern prefabricated building was provided when this station on the Yeovil-Exeter line near Exeter reopened. Because it has a short platform, some trains open only selected doors. The original station, known for nearly 100 years as Sidmouth junction, had closed in 1967 and the station building was demolished.
Feniton annual passenger numbers: 74,294

FERNHILL   Rhondda Cynon Taf   03 Oct 1988

This two-car platform station, subsequently extended to accommodate four cars, is on the reopened Aberdare branch.   Fernhill annual passenger numbers: 26,256

FILTON ABBEY WOOD South Gloucestershire   11 Mar 1996

This station with twin 97-metre platforms, ramp footbridge and shelters cost £1.5 million, funded jointly by Avon County Council, the Ministry of Defence (which has offices nearby), property developers and rail companies. Located between Bristol Parkway and Temple Meads, it is served by 60 trains a day and replaces the previous Filton station. In 2005 a third platform was added for improved services between Bristol and Wales.   Filton Abbey Wood annual passenger numbers: 1,021,550

FINNIESTON

See Exhibition Centre.

FISHGUARD AND GOODWICK Pembrokeshire   14 May 2012
ABERGWAUN AC WDIG *Sir Benfro*

Engineers lowered and realigned the track close to the platform at Goodwick. The existing Fishguard station at the ferry terminal was said to be too far from the town, 10 minutes walk away. Around £325,000 was spent to reopen the old station closer to the town. The Welsh Government agreed to fund five extra Monday-Saturday trains. Fishguard and Goodwick annual passenger numbers: 19,946

FITZWILLIAM West Yorkshire   01 Mar 1982

Two three-car platforms and a 24-space car park were provided on this new station near Wakefield on the line to Doncaster. The cost of £76,000 was met by West Yorkshire Passenger Transport Executive. A previous station nearby closed in 1967. Fitzwilliam annual passenger numbers: 292,918

FIVE WAYS West Midlands   08 May 1978

This is one of two new stations provided on the west suburban line. The cost of approximately £300,000 was met by West Midlands Passenger Transport Executive. The former station closed in 1944 and the location is now surrounded by business, shopping and housing areas. Five Ways annual passenger numbers: 1,585,886

FLOWERY FIELD Greater Manchester   13 May 1985

This station was newly opened experimentally to serve the Flowery Field area of Hyde on the Glossop line. Flowery Field annual passenger numbers: 197,330

FRIZINGHALL West Yorkshire   07 Sep 1987

This station, 3km from Bradford Forster Square, had been closed since 1965 and was reopened with staggered platforms on either side of a road bridge. It is served by

Bradford-Shipley trains and well patronised by pupils from nearby Bradford Grammar School.
Frizinghall annual passenger numbers: 376,850

G

GALASHIELS Selkirkshire   06 Sep 2015

Galashiels station was one of seven new stations on the reopened Borders Railway from Edinburgh Waverley to Tweedbank. The new single-platform Galashiels station is on the site of the old station, close to the town centre and the bus station.
See Chapter 4: New lines for passengers, Edinburgh-Tweedbank
Galashiels annual passenger numbers: 213,760

Picture: Borders Railway

BOWSHANK TUNNEL: Experts were brought in to help protect bats in 165-year-old Bowshank tunnel, 8km north of Galashiels. One-way bat flaps were installed so the bats could escape before Borders Railway reopening work started. No breeding or hibernation roosts were discovered but some Soprano pipistrelle and Myotis bats were found in the refuges used in the past by railway workers when trains passed. Alternative roost sites were provided nearby

43

GARSCADDEN Glasgow   07 Nov 1960

Situated on the Clydebank line, this station opened when the line was electrified.
Garscadden annual passenger numbers: 230,694

GARSDALE Cumbria   14 Jul 1986

Opened for Dalesrail services, this station reopened 16 years after closure and has
benefited from North Yorkshire County Council contributions for station improvements.
Garsdale annual passenger numbers: 15,684

GARSTON Hertfordshire   07 Feb 1966

This new station opened on the Watford Junction to St Albans Abbey line, which in
early 2010 was being considered for conversion to tram operation. The tram-train
scheme has been shelved, and the latest thinking is for a passing loop at Bricket Wood.
Garston (Hertfordshire) annual passenger numbers: 71,984

GARSTON Merseyside   03 Jan 1978

This station south-east of Liverpool was financed by funds from Merseyside Passenger
Transport Executive. In 2006 it was replaced by Liverpool South Parkway, which was
created from the former Allerton station after construction of new platforms.

GARTCOSH Glasgow   09 May 2005

This is a new station on the Glasgow Queen Street to Cumbernauld route. This
£3 million reopening was a joint project between Strathclyde Passenger Transport
Executive, North Lanarkshire Council and Scottish Enterprise. The previous station
closed in 1962.
Gartcosh annual passenger numbers: 156,776

GARTH Bridgend *Pen-y-bont ar Ogwr*   28 Sep 1992

A new single-platform station was built north of the site of a former station, named
Troedyrhiw Garth, which closed in 1970. It was one of six new stations for the Cardiff-
Maesteg service.
Garth annual passenger numbers: 12,796

GATESHEAD

See MetroCentre.

GILSHOCHILL Glasgow   03 Dec 1993

This station, funded by Strathclyde Regional Council, is on the Glasgow-Maryhill line. It

opened initially as Lambhill, but was renamed Gilshochill in 1998. The station is on the site of a former station closed in 1917.
Gilshochill annual passenger numbers: 86,996

GLAN CONWY Conwy   04 May 1970

This station on the Conwy Valley line, serving the village of Llansanffraid Glan Conwy, reopened six years after the original closure of Glan Conway station with its older spelling.
Glan Conwy annual passenger numbers: 3,748

GLASGOW CENTRAL Low Level Glasgow   05 Nov 1979

The two platforms were reopened to serve the electrified Argyle line, 15 years after the low-level services were withdrawn.
Glasgow Central annual passenger numbers 30,000,582

GLASSHOUGHTON West Yorkshire   21 Feb 2005

Leeds-Knottingley trains gained a new £2.3 million twin 97-metre platform station at Glasshoughton between Castleford and Pontefract Monkhill. On the site of the former Glasshoughton colliery, it is located close to Xscape ski and leisure complex, the Freeport shopping centre and the M62. The station includes digital CCTV, a customer information system, a public address system, cycle stands, a 100-space car park and an adjacent bus interchange. It was funded from Local Transport Plan sources with contributions of £250,000 from the Strategic Rail Authority and from the developers of the adjacent shopping centre.
Glasshoughton annual passenger numbers: 186,198

GLENROTHES WITH THORNTON Fife   11 May 1992

Funded by Fife Regional Council, Glenrothes Development Corporation and ScotRail, this station was opened after Fife Circle services had been reinstated. Glenrothes is a new town isolated from the rail system, and Thornton is the nearest practical railhead.
Glenrothes with Thornton annual passenger numbers: 76,688

GOLDTHORPE South Yorkshire   16 May 1988

Opened on the Sheffield-Pontefract line, the estimated cost of £180,000 was met partly by the South Yorkshire Passenger Transport Executive with a 50% grant from the European Community. Most services run from Sheffield to Leeds.
Goldthorpe annual passenger numbers: 62,510

GOLF STREET Angus   07 Nov 1960

This station was opened near Carnoustie on the Dundee-Aberdeen line at the initiative of local rail managers. However, bus deregulation and difficult connections resulted in

GRETNA GREEN: A simple bus shelter for well-dressed passengers in August 2016

poor patronage and since 1992 it has been served by only one train each way per day.
Golf Street annual passenger numbers: 168

GOREBRIDGE Midlothian   6 Sep 2015

Gorebridge was one of seven new stations on the reopened Borders Railway from
Edinburgh Waverley to Tweedbank. The new single-platform Gorebridge station is on
the site of the old station.
See Chapter 4: New lines for passengers, Edinburgh-Tweedbank
Gorebridge annual passenger numbers: 59,304

GREENFAULDS North Lanarkshire   15 May 1989

Opened on the Glasgow Queen Street to Cumbernauld line at a cost of £180,000,
funded by Strathclyde Regional Council.
Greenfaulds annual passenger numbers: 130,914

GRETNA GREEN Dumfries and Galloway   20 Sep 1993

Reopened on the Nith Valley, Carlisle-Dumfries line with funding from Dumfries and
Galloway Regional Council, the station was built as a single platform on the site of the
original station which closed in 1965.
Gretna Green annual passenger numbers: 38,940

GYPSY LANE Redcar and Cleveland   03 May 1976

Costing £24,000, this new station was opened on the line from Whitby to
Middlesbrough.
Gypsy Lane annual passenger numbers: 30,338

HACKNEY CENTRAL Greater London **12 May 1980**

This North London line station was rebuilt slightly west of the former station of the same name. It reopened at a cost of £300,000 with funds provided by the Greater London Council.
Hackney Central annual passenger numbers: 5,978,530

HACKNEY WICK Greater London **12 May 1980**

This station, east of Hackney Central and Homerton stations on the North London line, was opened with funding from the Greater London Council. It was renovated and provided with disabled access ramps in late 2004. The station is undergoing a £25 million improvement programme in 2017 with a new subway and lifts to replace the existing footbridge and ramps. The work is linked to a major redevelopment around the station. The train service is operated by London Overground.
Hackney Wick annual passenger numbers: 2,103,982

HADDENHAM & THAME PARKWAY Bucks **03 Oct 1987**

This single-platform station, opened north of the former Haddenham station, reducing the long gap between Bicester North and Princes Risborough. With parking for 180 cars it serves a population catchment of 25,000. The £430,000 cost was aided by a £72,000 contribution from Oxfordshire and Buckinghamshire county councils. Thame town

Picture: Network Rail

HACKNEY WICK: Major work was under way in 2017 to provide a subway

is 6km to the west in Oxfordshire. With the restoration of double track early in 1998 (Evergreen Phase 1), a new twin platform station was built.
Haddenham & Thame Parkway annual passenger numbers: 803,904

HAG FOLD Greater Manchester   11 May 1987

An experimental station, opened to serve Atherton on the Wigan to Manchester Victoria line. The twin timber platforms cost £157,000, funded by Greater Manchester Passenger Transport Executive.   Hag Fold annual passenger numbers: 51,582

HAGGERSTON Greater London   27 Apr 2010

The original 1865 North London Railway station closed in 1940. It reopened on the opposite, north side of Lee Street, in 2010 as part of the London Overground's East London line.
See Chapter 4: New lines for passengers, East London line
Haggerston annual passenger numbers: 3,187,120

HALEWOOD Merseyside   16 May 1988

This £440,000 station opened to serve 10,000 people within a 1km radius. It is on the City line (Liverpool-Warrington-Manchester) between Hunts Cross and Hough Green.
Halewood annual passenger numbers: 117,560

HALL I' TH' WOOD Greater Manchester   29 Sep 1986

Opened experimentally for £120,000, this station on the Bolton-Blackburn line was funded by Greater Manchester Passenger Transport Executive. It is in the middle of a housing estate and takes its name from a 16th century manor house, now a museum.
Hall I'Th'Wood annual passenger numbers: 116,428

HATTERSLEY Greater Manchester   08 May 1978

Opened by Greater Manchester Passenger Transport Executive on the Manchester to Glossop and Hadfield line.
Hattersley annual passenger numbers: 64,320

HAWKHEAD Renfrewshire   12 Apr 1991

Opened as an additional station on the reopened Paisley Canal line, this station has a single platform and cost £127,000, funded by Strathclyde Regional Council.
Hawkhead annual passenger numbers: 201,256

HEATHROW CENTRAL Greater London   25 May 1998

Serving airport terminals 1,2 and 3, this sub-surface station has two 180-metre platforms and is on the BAA's Paddington-Heathrow express service. The station,

48

which does not belong to Network Rail, opened as part of the £300 million Heathrow Express project, which includes construction of a 6.5km tunnel, new flyovers at Hayes junction, electrification of the 25km route to Paddington, and a fleet of new trains. The airport station was officially opened by prime minister Tony Blair. The station is 6.5km 'down-tunnel' from the junction with the Great Western main line. In 1998, a temporary surface-level station called Heathrow Junction at Stockley Park was in operation after the 1994 collapse of a tunnel during construction. Buses provided the final link.
Heathrow Express estimate of annual passenger use: 5,800,000

HEATHROW TERMINAL 4 Greater London   25 May 1998

This station is the terminus of the new Paddington-Heathrow express route on the south side of Heathrow. The four trains per hour service offers a 22-minute journey at 145km/h. Additional Heathrow Connect services were added in 2004.

HEATHROW TERMINAL 5 Greater London   27 Mar 2008

This station is connected to the existing Heathrow railway line by two 1.7km tunnels. Completed in mid-2007, it consists of six platforms, two for Heathrow Express, two for the Piccadilly line Underground trains and the remaining two for a future extension.

HEDGE END Hampshire   14 May 1990

Hedge End station near Eastleigh is situated on the Eastleigh-Fareham line which was newly electrified in 1990. Eastleigh Borough Council contributed £350,000 to this substantial two-platform station, which has a large car parking area.
Hedge End annual passenger numbers: 508,982

HEDNESFORD Staffordshire   08 Apr 1989

The remaining southbound platform of the original station which closed in 1965 was refurbished as the terminus of an experimental hourly service from Walsall. The service promptly achieved 50% above break-even passenger levels and in 1997 a new northbound platform opened for Rugeley trains.
Hednesford annual passenger numbers: 166,954

HEWORTH Tyne and Wear   Nov 1979

Heworth station is 4km from Newcastle Central on the line to Sunderland and opened to British Rail trains in 1979, and to Metro trains two years later. It has an adjacent bus station.
Heworth annual passenger numbers: 18,898 (not including Metro passengers)

HEYSHAM PORT Lancashire   11 May 1987

When it reopened 12 years after it had closed, trains ran from Manchester to connect with Isle of Man ferries at this station, which uses just one platform. It was initially called

49

Heysham Harbour. British Rail met the operating expenses, and the £60,000 cost of the station came from Lancaster City Council, Isle of Man Steam Packet Company and Lancashire County Council.   Heysham Port annual passenger numbers: 9,128

HOMERTON Greater London   13 May 1985

At a cost of £444,000, this reconstructed station on the North London line was funded by the Greater London Council.   Homerton annual passenger numbers: 4,652,282

HONEYBOURNE Worcestershire   25 May 1981

With minimal expenditure, a single platform was reopened on the Oxford-Worcester Cotswold line after a campaign by the Cotswold Line Promotion Group. Another platform was added in 2011 when the line was redoubled. The original four-platform station closed in 1969.
See Chapter 3: Stations opening soon, Broadway
Honeybourne annual passenger numbers: 57,978

HORNBEAM PARK North Yorkshire   24 Aug 1992

The £413,000 cost of this new two-platform station was shared between Harrogate Borough Council, North Yorkshire County Council, Harrogate College, Hornbeam Business Park, ICI, the Homeowners' Friendly Society and Regional Railways. It has an 80-space car park. In 2006 the borough council entered into an agreement with the Hornbeam Park Development Company to provide better facilities including toilets and a newspaper kiosk.   Hornbeam Park annual passenger numbers: 352,614

HORTON-IN-RIBBLESDALE North Yorkshire   14 Jul 1986

This station reopened 16 years after it had closed, with the help of grants from North Yorkshire County Council and Craven District Council, following the success of the Dalesrail charter services run since 1974.
Horton-in-Ribblesdale annual passenger numbers: 16,096

HORWICH PARKWAY Greater Manchester   30 May 1999

Located between Blackrod and Lostock on the Preston-Manchester line, this is a new 400-metre twin-platform station. In addition to offering a park-and-ride facility, the station serves Bolton Wanderers' football stadium as well as a retail and leisure complex. The £3.6 million construction cost was met by funding contributions from Greater Manchester Passenger Transport Authority, local developers and the football club. In 2006 a new ticket office was officially opened by the local MP Ruth Kelly, who had also opened the station originally. From 2012, the station became one of Britain's few stations to be powered by a wind turbine (Corrour in Scotland was the first). The car park has been extended to accommodate 250 cars.
Horwich Parkway annual passenger numbers: 599,916

HOWWOOD Renfrewshire 12 Mar 2001

Situated on the Glasgow-Ayr line between Lochwinnoch and Milliken Park, this station's twin 312-metre platforms cost £1.25 million and were funded by Strathclyde Passenger Transport Executive with a £100,000 contribution from development company Bellway Homes. An earlier station had closed in 1955.
Howwood annual passenger numbers: 124,886

HOW WOOD Hertfordshire 22 Oct 1988

The four-car platform opened on the Watford to St Albans Abbey branch following £81,000 funding from Hertfordshire County Council and the local parish council.
How Wood annual passenger numbers: 27,804

HOXTON Greater London 27 Apr 2010

Hoxton is a completely new station built as part of the London Overground's East London line. It is close to the Geffrye Museum. Hoxton station become the new location for the North London Railway war memorial which was rededicated on Remembrance Sunday 2011.
See Chapter 4: New lines for passengers, East London line
Hoxton annual passenger numbers: 2,931,902

HUCKNALL Nottinghamshire 08 May 1993

The first Fun Day trains called at this new platform, followed by regular services from 17 May 1993 linking Nottingham and Newstead in Phase 1 on the Robin Hood line scheme. It is also a tram stop for Nottingham Express Transit. There is a large car park at the station which provides park-and-ride services. The original station closed in 1964.
Hucknall annual passenger numbers: 150,620

HUMPHREY PARK Greater Manchester 15 Oct 1984

This experimentally opened station cost £86,000 and is located on the Warrington-Manchester line.
Humphrey Park annual passenger numbers: 35,070

HYNDLAND Glasgow 07 Nov 1960

The station opened following electrification of the Airdrie to Helensburgh line, and replaced the old Hyndland terminal station.
Hyndland annual passenger numbers: 1,743,602

I

IBM Inverclyde   08 May 1978

Opened on the Wemyss Bay electrified line and funded by British Rail, Strathclyde
Regional Council and the computer company IBM. It was earlier called IBM Halt.
IBM annual passenger numbers: 22,016

ILKESTON Derbyshire   02 Apr 2017

With a population of 40,000, Ilkeston was one of the largest towns in England without
a station. Hundreds of people turned up on Sunday 2 April 2017 when trains began
calling at the new station on the Erewash line between Derby and Chesterfield.
A day of celebration took place in July 2017 when it was reported that more than
30,000 people used the station in the first three months. Derbyshire County Council
contributed nearly £3 million to the £10 million cost and nearly £7 million came from
the Government's new station fund. Funding was agreed in 2013 but construction
was hindered by the discovery of protected newts and the need to make provision for
the possibility of flooding. The newts had to be trapped and relocated. The car park
has only 90 spaces because the cost of preventing the car park from flooding was
considered too high. The new station is on the site of the Ilkeston Junction and Cossall
station that closed in 1967 and is on the existing Erewash Valley railway line, only 3km
from the M1 motorway. The station has an hourly Northern service, with long-distance
Norwich-Nottingham-Liverpool trains also calling. MP Maggie Throup said: "We have
finally cast off the dubious title of the largest town in Britain without a station. This is a
truly historic moment in the life of our town and already we are beginning to reap the
benefits." It was the culmination of a 24-year campaign by Ilkeston Rail Action Group
which first met in a nearby pub in 1993.

IMPERIAL WHARF Greater London   27 Sep 2009

This £7.8 million London Overground station near Chelsea Harbour on the West London
line provides a direct link to Britain's busiest rail interchange, Clapham Junction, to the
south, and Willesden Junction to the north. Developers St George contributed
£4.8 million towards the cost. The Royal Borough of Kensington and Chelsea gave
£600,000, along with £1.35 million from the London Borough of Hammersmith and
Fulham. Transport for London paid £1 million.
Imperial Wharf annual passenger numbers: 3,290,200

ISLIP Oxfordshire   26 Oct 2015

The single-platform station closed on 15 February 2014 to allow upgrading of the line

Picture: East Midlands Trains

ILKESTON: Passengers lined up to greet the first train to stop at Ilkeston for 50 years

between Oxford and Bicester for Chiltern Railways' new London Marylebone to Oxford service. The rebuilt double-platform station reopened on 26 October 2015. It was a second reopening for Islip, with the first taking place in May 1989. Funded by British Rail along with Oxfordshire County and Oxford City councils, the £72,000 single-platform station opened two years after the Oxford-Bicester Town train service was reinstated and 21 years after the original station had closed in 1968.
See Chapter 4: New lines for passengers, Bicester-Oxford Parkway
Islip annual passenger numbers: 101,482

IVYBRIDGE Devon   14 Jul 1994

This £1.5 million station, 18km east of Plymouth, was co-funded by Devon County Council, Plymouth City Council and South Hams District Council with contributions from the European Union. It has two 108-metre platforms, a ramped footbridge, a large car park and a bus-turning circle. The original station closed in 1959.
Ivybridge annual passenger numbers: 53,020

JAMES COOK UNIVERSITY HOSPITAL Middlesbrough **17 May 2014**

Plans for the new station were discussed for 25 years! The new £2.2 million single-platform station is a five to 10 minute walk from the hospital and is on the Esk Valley line linking Middlesbrough to Whitby via Nunthorpe. The station was jointly funded by the Department for Transport and the Tees Valley local enterprise partnership and was aimed at cutting car use in the area.

James Cook University Hospital annual passenger numbers: 31,578

JEWELLERY QUARTER West Midlands   **24 Sep 1995**

One of three new stations built to complete reinstatement of the Birmingham Snow Hill route, this £2.5 million station is at the west portal of Hockley tunnel. The twin platforms are 150 metres long. An interchange with the parallel Midland Metro service opened in 1999.

Jewellery Quarter annual passenger numbers: 427,182

Picture: Network Rail

JAMES COOK UNIVERSITY HOSPITAL: Baroness Kramer at the opening ceremony

KELVINDALE Glasgow   29 Sep 2005

The station, built on a new line linking the existing Anniesland and Maryhill stations, was opened ahead of schedule. The new line and station, including a new bay platform at Anniesland, form part of the £35 million Larkhall-Milngavie project to improve access between north and south Glasgow. The station was to have been called Dawsholm.
See Chapter 4: New lines for passengers, Maryhill-Anniesland
Kelvindale annual passenger numbers: 91,570

KENTISH TOWN WEST Greater London   05 Oct 1981

This North London line station, 1.5km from Gospel Oak, was opened using a £400,000 grant from the Greater London Council. An earlier station closed after a fire in 1971.
Kentish Town West annual passenger numbers: 2,011,132

KILMAURS East Ayrshire   12 May 1984

This reopened station is just north of Kilmarnock on the Glasgow-Dumfries line. It cost £238,000 and was funded by Strathclyde Regional Council. An earlier station had closed in 1966.
Kilmaurs annual passenger numbers: 103,478

KINGS CROSS THAMESLINK Greater London   11 Jul 1983

This station, with an entrance on Pentonville Road, opened in 1983 as Kings Cross Midland, part of the Midland Electrics (Bedford-Moorgate) project. Kings Cross (Met), on the same site, had closed in 1979. In 1988 Kings Cross Midland was renamed Kings Cross Thameslink, after the Thameslink route to Blackfriars and Brighton was created. It was a few minutes walk from King's Cross main line station, and was also connected by a 600-metre tunnel to the Victoria and Piccadilly Underground platforms. Consisting of twin eight-car platforms (called A and B) which could not easily be extended to allow for 12-car trains and did not meet minimum width standards, it closed in 2007 when two new low-level platforms opened at London St Pancras.

KINGSKNOWE Edinburgh   01 Feb 1971

This two-platform station, near Edinburgh on the Glasgow-Edinburgh via Shotts line, was reopened as a result of a local campaign following closure in 1964.
Kingsknowe annual passenger numbers: 20,150

KIRKBY-IN-ASHFIELD Nottinghamshire   17 Nov 1996

Opened on a Sunday for Fun Day services, this new two-platform station joined others built in 1993 and 1995 on the Robin Hood line. It is in a cutting with access via ramps. Kirkby-in-Ashfield annual passenger numbers: 26,786

KIRKBY STEPHEN Cumbria   14 Jul 1986

Dalesrail services prompted the reopening of this two-platform station, formerly known as Kirkby Stephen West, with the help of funds from the parish council and Cumbria County Council. Like many stations on the route it had closed in May 1970. Kirkby Stephen annual passenger numbers: 177,474

KIRK SANDALL South Yorkshire   13 May 1991

This two-platform station is 6km north-east of Doncaster on the Doncaster-Hull line. Kirk Sandall annual passenger numbers: 128,484

KIRKSTALL FORGE Leeds   19 June 2016

The new station is on a busy stretch of line between Leeds and Shipley and is on a former industrial site. It serves a £400 million development of 1,000 new homes, plus

offices and shops. The Government contributed £9 million to the cost, with £1.4 million from the West Yorkshire Combined Authority. Commercial Estates Group contributed £5 million. The station is five kilometres from Leeds city centre and when it opened, the leader of Leeds City Council, Councillor Judith Blake said: "The station has a key role to play in realising the major regeneration potential of the broader Kirkstall Forge development, bringing with it new jobs, training opportunities, housing and a range of office and leisure facilities to offer a significant boost to the local economy." By spring 2017, patronage had already exceeded expectations.

KIRKWOOD North Lanarkshire   04 Oct 1993

This is one of five stations reopened with Strathclyde Regional Council funding when the freight-only Glasgow-Whifflet line was restored for passenger use.
Kirkwood annual passenger numbers: 138,888

L

LAKE Isle of Wight   11 May 1987

This £80,000 station is served by former London Underground trains and is near the site of an earlier halt between Sandown and Shanklin. It opened with a contribution of £30,000 from Isle of Wight County Council.
Lake annual passenger numbers: 52,310

LAMBHILL

See Gilshochill.

LANDYWOOD Staffordshire   08 Apr 1989

A two-platform station with new staggered platforms was opened for Walsall-Hednesford trains on this former freight-only route. One of six stations reopened on the Cannock Chase line, Landywood was built on a new site 1km south of the former Great Wyrley station to serve a large housing development.
Landywood annual passenger numbers: 97,214

LANGHO Lancashire   29 May 1994

A two-platform station, 8km north of Blackburn, reopened for new services on the Blackburn-Clitheroe line, 32 years after the original station had closed.
Langho annual passenger numbers: 35,734

LANGLEY MILL Derbyshire   12 May 1986

This station is on the Sheffield-Nottingham line and has twin 92-metre platforms, plus a car park. The £130,000 cost was met by £78,000 from Derbyshire County

Council, £26,000 from Nottinghamshire County Council, £19,000 from Amber Valley District Council and the remainder from two parish councils. The original station had closed in 1967.
Langley Mill annual passenger numbers: 115,686

LANGWATHBY Cumbria   14 Jul 1986

Cumbria County Council funded the cost of reopening this two-platform station on the Settle-Carlisle line for Dalesrail trains. The station had closed in 1970.
Langwathby annual passenger numbers: 17,870

LANGWITH-WHALEY THORNS Derbyshire   24 May 1998

Costing £600,000, this station, north of Shirebrook on Phase 3 of the 21km Robin Hood line linking Mansfield and Worksop, has twin 79-metre platforms. It serves the village of Whaley Thorns and the more extensive Langwith area. The original Langwith station had closed in 1964.
See Chapter 4: New lines for passengers, Robin Hood line
Langwith-Whaley Thorns annual passenger numbers: 22,292

LARKHALL South Lanarkshire   12 Dec 2005

This two-platform terminal station, on the reopened branch line south east of Glasgow from Haughhead junction near Hamilton, serves a population of 14,000. The new Monday to Saturday service started with a 30-minute frequency, but following higher than predicted patronage, a Sunday service was introduced in December 2007. The previous passenger service had been withdrawn in 1965. The new route, which improves rail access to the south of Glasgow, is part of the £35 million Larkhall-Milngavie scheme.
Larkhall annual passenger numbers: 420,366

LAURENCEKIRK Aberdeenshire   18 May 2009

The 1848 grade B listed building on the northbound platform of the station, which closed in 1967, has been restored to become the main station facility. There are ticket machines, a customer information system, CCTV and a footbridge with a ramp. A 70-space car park was built in the nearby industrial estate. The £3.24 million cost was funded by Transport Scotland (80%) and NESTRANS, the NE Scotland Transport Agency. On weekdays, nine trains to Aberdeen call, and 10 to Dundee. The decision to reopen was announced by Deputy First Minister Nicol Stephen, formerly Transport Minister at the Scottish Executive. As MSP for Aberdeen South he had campaigned for this reopening for many years. For the first six weeks after reopening, use of the station was 80% above the predicted level. The theoretical forecast was for 36,000 passengers per annum.
Laurencekirk annual passenger numbers: 104,488

WELCOME: The first train to call at Laurencekirk for more than 40 years was greeted by an enthusiastic crowd. Use of the station was 80% higher than expected

LAZONBY & KIRKOSWALD Cumbria   14 Jul 1986

The station closed in 1970. Following the success of the Dalesrail charter trains which started in May 1974, it reopened to a regular train service in 1986, thanks to financial support from Cumbria County Council.
Lazonby & Kirkoswald annual passenger numbers: 12,510

LEA BRIDGE Greater London   16 May 2016

The station was closed by stealth in 1985 after several years of a timetable so bizarre as to be virtually useless. The rebuilt £6.5 million station was backed by Waltham Forest Council because it will promote widespread generation "in a large area of deprivation". The station is a few minutes by rail from the Olympic park and Westfield shopping centre at Stratford. The rail journey to Stratford takes five minutes, compared with up to 45 minutes by bus. The station is served by the half-hourly service between Stratford and Bishops Stortford/Stansted Airport. There are also proposals to provide a 15-minute interval service between Stratford and Angel Road where there is a big IKEA store. When the old station closed, Railfuture member Graham Larkbey performed at Lea Bridge station on the last day with his band Aunt Fortescue's Bluesrockers. The

LEA BRIDGE: Railfuture campaigner Peter Woodrow, Greater London Assembly member Jennette Arnold, left, and Stella Creasey MP at the opening of the station

band re-formed and played again for the reopening day. Railfuture campaigned for years for the reopening, as well as funding a consultant's report. By March 2017, use of the station had exceeded expectations by 30%.

LEA GREEN Merseyside   17 Sep 2000

This £2.7 million station opened with the benefit of £700,000 from the European Regional Development Fund, £200,000 from Single Regeneration Budget funding and £1.3 million from Merseytravel. Situated between Rainhill and St Helens junction, the station serves a large employment area and has a 190-space car park. The original closed in 1955.

Lea Green annual passenger numbers: 439,500

LELANT SALTINGS Cornwall   23 May 1978

This station with one platform and a large car park provides a park-and-ride facility to relieve summer traffic congestion in St Ives.
Lelant Saltings annual passenger numbers: 125,064

LICHFIELD TRENT VALLEY High Level Staffs   28 Nov 1988

The existing northbound platform was refurbished and reopened as a new northern terminus for the Cross-City service with a £5,000 contribution from Lichfield District Council. The low level platforms are on the West Coast main line.
Lichfield Trent Valley annual passenger numbers: 1,063,986

LISVANE & THORNHILL Cardiff   04 Nov 1985
LLYSFAEN   *Caerdydd*

This two-platform station on the Rhymney Valley line cost £181,000. It replaced the tiny request stop Cefn Onn Halt which closed in 1986.
Lisvane & Thornhill annual passenger numbers: 211,870

LIVERPOOL CENTRAL Deep Level Merseyside   02 May 1977

Opened with one platform on the single loop line tunnel for Wirral trains, with new entrances. The combined station, below the site of a former main line terminus, is now the busiest in Liverpool, allowing travellers to interchange between the Wirral and Northern lines.   Liverpool Central total annual passenger numbers: 15,638,894

LIVERPOOL LIME STREET Low Level Merseyside   30 Oct 1977

Situated under Liverpool's main line terminal station, this new underground station was built to serve trains running clockwise on the new loop line to and from the Wirral.
Liverpool Lime Street annual passenger numbers: 15,227,344

LIVERPOOL SOUTH PARKWAY Merseyside   11 Jun 2006

This £32 million station was created by merging Garston and Allerton stations into a rail, bus and park-and-ride facility with an integrated booking office, 240-space free car park with CCTV, a 16-space taxi rank, 61 secure cycle parking spaces, fully accessible lifts and comfortable, warm waiting areas. The station, which was designed to be environmentally friendly, with solar photovoltaic cells on the south facing windows and facilities for harvesting rainwater, is served by a bus to Liverpool John Lennon Airport. Funding consisted of £6 million from the Department for Transport, £11 million from the European Regional Development Fund, £1 million from Liverpool City Council and the remainder from Merseytravel. By autumn 2008 passenger numbers stood at 26,000 a week, compared to the combined 10,000 a week from the former stations. By 2010 it

LIVERPOOL SOUTH PARKWAY: This environmentally friendly station replaced Garston and Allerton stations and also serves Liverpool John Lennon Airport

had risen to 32,700. The car park was fully occupied every day. In 2009, after passenger numbers had grown to 4,000 a day, Merseytravel funded an £850,000 project to provide a travel centre, waiting room, cycle storage and ticket gates compatible with smart-card ticketing. An additional 60 car park spaces were also built. See GARSTON Merseyside.
Liverpool South Parkway annual passenger numbers: 1,893,958

LIVINGSTON NORTH West Lothian   24 Mar 1986

Opened experimentally as part of the Bathgate line reopening, this station was funded by Lothian Regional Council, West Lothian District Council, Livingston Development Corporation, the Scottish Development Agency and the European Regional Development Fund. It is close to the former Livingston station which closed in 1948.
Livingston North annual passenger numbers: 1,155,046

LIVINGSTON SOUTH West Lothian   06 Oct 1984

Opened on the Glasgow-Edinburgh via Shotts line at a cost of £293,000, to which Livingston Development Corporation contributed £195,000.
Livingston South annual passenger numbers: 342,770

LLANDECWYN Gwynedd   01 Sep 2014

British Rail planned to close Llandecwyn station in the 1990s but the service survived.
The two-coach long single-platform station was however completely rebuilt at a new
location in 2014 as part of a comprehensive plan to replace Pont Briwet (road and rail).
The rail track was realigned for the new bridge and the rail service was suspended for
nearly a year while the bridge was rebuilt.
Llandecwyn annual passenger numbers 2,370

LLANFAIRPWLL Isle of Anglesey   07 May 1973

Llanfairpwllgwyngyllgogerychwyrndrobwllllantysiliogogogoch Sir Ynys Môn

This two-platform station, which originally closed in 1966, is on the Anglesey side of
Britannia Bridge on the line to Holyhead. It carries the longest station name in Britain!
Also known as Llanfair PG, Network Rail refers to it as Llanfairpwll. The station reopened
temporarily in May 1970 and closed again in January 1972.
Llanfairpwll annual passenger numbers: 18,482

LLANHARAN *Rhondda Cynon Taf*   10 Dec 2007

This £4.3 million station is located between Pontyclun and Pencoed in South Wales. It is
served by trains to Cardiff, Bridgend and Maesteg. Construction, which started in March
2007, took nine months. The station has a footbridge, passenger information displays,
help points, CCTV and a car park. It is built on the site of the original station, which
closed in 1964.
Llanharan annual passenger numbers: 169,428

LLANHILLETH Blaenau Gwent   27 Apr 2008
LLANHILEDD

Llanhilleth was the fifth new station opened on the Ebbw Valley line, two months after
the line reopened. It has a single platform and a car park.
Llanhilleth annual passenger numbers: 80,090

LLANRWST Conwy   29 Jul 1989

The former Llanrwst station was renamed North Llanrwst when this new station was
built 1.5km further south and sited closer to the town centre, more convenient for
residents and tourists.
Llanrwst annual passenger numbers: 13,888

LLANSAMLET Swansea *Abertawe*   27 Jun 1994

Served by Swanline trains, this two-platform station is located between Swansea and
Neath. The original closed in 1964.
Llansamlet annual passenger numbers: 33,862

LLANTWIT MAJOR   Vale of Glamorgan   12 Jun 2005
LLANILLTUD FAWR *Bro Morgannwg*

This is one of two new stations opened on the Vale of Glamorgan line. The line, providing an alternative route between Cardiff and Bridgend had, since 1964, been used only for freight traffic plus diverted passenger services caused by engineering work. The total cost of the scheme, which included a reinstated and extended four-car bay platform at Bridgend, 5.5km of new rail, the line being upgraded for almost 100km/h running and seven new signals, was £17 million and was funded by the Welsh Government. Before opening, it had been predicted that most passenger journeys would be eastwards to Cardiff, but in fact a significant proportion of travellers head west for Bridgend, showing once again that transport consultants often underestimate demand for local rail travel. An estimated 225,000 passenger journeys were made along the line in the first 12 months.
Llantwit Major annual passenger numbers: 304,630

LOCH AWE   Argyll and Bute   01 May 1985

This station on the Oban line opened on an experimental basis. An earlier station had closed in 1965.
Loch Awe annual passenger numbers: 4,804

LOCH EIL OUTWARD BOUND   Fort William   06 May 1985

Opened experimentally on the Fort William-Mallaig line, its name refers to the Outward Bound centre nearby.
Loch Eil Outward Bound annual passenger numbers: 478

LOCHWINNOCH   Renfrewshire   27 Jun 1966

Reopened as Lochside after being closed in 1955, this station on the Glasgow-Ayr line served Lochwinnoch after the closure of the loop line which ran through Lochwinnoch and several other small towns. It was renamed Lochwinnoch in 1985.
Lochwinnoch annual passenger numbers: 202,948

LONDON FIELDS   Greater London   29 Sep 1986

Having been destroyed by fire on Friday 13 November 1981, this station was restored and reopened five years later. It lies just south of Hackney Downs station on the Liverpool Street to Enfield line.
London Fields annual passenger numbers: 1,184,294

LONDON ST PANCRAS INTERNATIONAL   14 Nov 2007

St Pancras International is now the terminus for Eurostar trains in Britain. It was opened officially by the Queen on 7 November 2007 and opened for passengers on 14 November. Eurostars were transferred from London Waterloo to St Pancras, which was modernised at a cost of £800 million. The original curved roof Victorian station is now used exclusively by Eurostars which share the new flat-roof extension with inter-city domestic services to the Midlands and high-speed services to Kent. Eurostar estimates around 10,000,000 passengers per year

LONDON ST PANCRAS Low level   09 Dec 2007

Building the low-level part of St Pancras main line station as a concrete box was started in 2004, and required the temporary severing of Thameslink services. It was completed in 2005. The fit-out of the 12-car platforms – called A and B – had to wait until January 2006 for Department for Transport approval of the £78 million cost. The new low level station allowed the cramped Kings Cross Thameslink station in Pentonville Road to be closed on 8 December 2007, although part of it is still used as an entrance to the London Underground. London St Pancras total annual passenger numbers: 31,723,686

LONDON WATERLOO INTERNATIONAL   14 Nov 1994

This £130 million five-platform wing of Waterloo station (numbered from 20 to 24 with platform lengths varying between 396 metres and 428 metres) was built on two former Windsor line platforms and carriage sidings. The complex, which was designed by Nicholas Grimshaw, was complete on 17 May 1993 but had to wait for the Eurostar services to start more than a year later. The structure is on four levels: platforms, departures/arrivals, customs and immigration and car park (basement). The station, which increased its service from an initial four international trains each way per day in 1994 to 25 in 2007, ceased serving Eurostar trains on 13 Nov 2007 when they transferred to St Pancras International. The station will be retained for domestic services. A phased reopening is dependent on remodelling work on the main station platforms, especially lengthening platforms 1-4). The international station is expected to be back in use for domestic services in late 2017.

LONGBECK Redcar and Cleveland   13 May 1985

Sited between Marske and Redcar East on the Saltburn-Middlesbrough line, the new station at Longbeck was opened following an investment of £100,000 by Cleveland County Council.   Longbeck annual passenger numbers: 43,170

LONGBRIDGE West Midlands   08 May 1978

This new station was opened for the new cross-city service linking Lichfield and Redditch. The station, which cost £300,000 has twin nine-car platforms and a covered footbridge.   Longbridge annual passenger numbers: 919,184

LOSTOCK Greater Manchester   16 May 1988

This station is west of Bolton on the Preston line. In 2006, Network Rail suggested adding a third platform to allow a more frequent service. The Bolton-Wigan branch line

diverges just south of Lostock's platforms, but there are currently no platforms on the branch to Wigan and Southport. Lostock Junction station had closed in 1967.
Lostock annual passenger numbers: 41,510

LOSTOCK HALL Lancashire   14 May 1984

At a cost of £110,000 to Lancashire County Council, this station on the Preston-Blackburn line reopened on an experimental basis. The original station closed in 1971.
Lostock Hall annual passenger numbers: 232,442

LOW MOOR Bradford   02 Apr 2017

Even before Low Moor station opened in 2017, a Friends group was formed. They want the hourly Leeds-Halifax-Huddersfield service and the Bradford-London Grand Central trains to be supplemented by direct trains to Manchester. Low Moor serves Wyke and Oakenshaw and is now the closest rail link to Cleckheaton. Councillor Keith Wakefield, chairman of the West Yorkshire Combined Authority transport committee, said: "Its proximity to the M62 and M606 will attract park-and-ride users which will help reduce city centre congestion. Low Moor will also generate significant economic and social benefits by attracting new jobs and investment."
Work started on building the new £10.8 million station in 2015 but the discovery of a 200-year-old mine shaft delayed construction. The station, on a curve in the Calder Valley line, also provides access for cyclists and walkers to the eight-mile Spen Valley Greenway to Cleckheaton, Heckmondwike and Ravensthorpe on a former rail line. The previous Low Moor station was closed in 1965 and demolished, but West

LOW MOOR: Paul Barnfield of Northern Trains, left, with Councillor Eric Firth, Network Rail's Paul Rutter, Councillor Keith Wakefield, Councillor Andrew Pinnock, Councillor Sarah Ferriby, Counciller Val Slater, Councillor David Warburton and MP Judith Cummins at the opening of the station

Yorkshire Combined Authority expects more than 500,000 passengers a year to use the new station. The Halifax and District Rail Action Group is now campaigning for the reopening of Elland station which is 10 kilometres away.

LUTON AIRPORT PARKWAY Bedfordshire   21 Nov 1999

Costing £12.5 million and sited 1.5km south of Luton station, this four-platform facility has parking for 1,000 cars, as well as lifts and escalators. It provides a major park-and-ride facility from the nearby M1 and a useful transport link for 1.5 million air travellers annually. The station was funded by Railtrack together with a £2.8 million contribution from the local authority. The station was built with eight-car platforms, which meant some inter-city services could not call there. However, the lines were slewed to accommodate the island platforms which meant that each platform could be extended by 80 metres to support the 12-coach services resulting from the £5,500 million Thameslink upgrade programme which should be complete by 2018. The platform extensions were finished in 2008.
Luton Airport Parkway annual passenger numbers: 3,188,146

LYMPSTONE COMMANDO Devon   03 May 1976

This station, on the Exeter-Exmouth line, was opened to serve the Royal Marine training base.
Lympstone Commando annual passenger numbers: 54,026

MAESTEG Bridgend *Pen-y-bont ar Ogwr*   28 Sep 1992

A 14km stretch of single-track freight line benefited from a £3.3 million grant from Mid Glamorgan County Council and the European Development Fund, to provide six new stations and three class 143 diesel trains which run from Cardiff via Bridgend. The Maesteg platform was sited south of the former Castle Street station, near a car park and rail-link bus service to Caerau. Maesteg lost its passenger service in 1970.
Maesteg annual passenger numbers: 184,906

MAESTEG EWENNY ROAD Bridgend   26 Oct 1992
Pen-y-bont ar Ogwr

This completely new station opened south of the town centre to serve local housing and industry. It was one of six new stations for Cardiff-Maesteg services.
Maesteg Ewenny Road annual passenger numbers: 4,426

MANCHESTER AIRPORT Greater Manchester   17 May 1993

This £27 million station, its style in keeping with the international airport it serves, is at the end of a new 2.5km electrified branch off the Styal line for train services to and from Manchester Piccadilly. Network Rail awarded a £15 million contract for a third eight-car platform which was jointly funded by NR, Greater Manchester Passenger Transport Authority (around £5 million) and The Northern Way (a collaboration between the three northern regional development agencies). The cost was high because of a deep cutting. The new platform was opened in 2008. A fourth platform was added in 2014 at a cost of £20 million. There is a long-term proposal to turn the line into a through route, and Manchester Metrolink also now serves the airport.
Manchester Airport annual passenger numbers: 3,632,308

MANSFIELD Nottinghamshire   20 Nov 1995

This new station opened as part of the £20 million Robin Hood line Phase 2, to serve Mansfield town centre. The original station closed in 1964.
See Chapter 4: New lines for passengers, Robin Hood line
Mansfield annual passenger numbers: 394,640

MANSFIELD WOODHOUSE Nottinghamshire   20 Nov 1995

This station utilises a former goods warehouse which straddles the bay platform and track. It opened as a terminus for the Phase 2 extension of the Robin Hood line.
See Chapter 4: New lines for passengers, Robin Hood line
Mansfield Woodhouse annual passenger numbers: 169,506

MARTINS HERON Berkshire   03 Oct 1988

Located between Ascot and Bracknell, this £500,000 station on the London Waterloo to Reading main line was jointly funded by Berkshire County Council and British Rail.
Martins Heron annual passenger numbers: 588,416

MARYHILL Glasgow   03 Dec 1993

Opened as part of the Maryhill to Glasgow north suburban diesel service, this station was funded by Strathclyde Regional Council. In 2005 a new 1.5km line was built to connect Maryhill to Anniesland, with a new station at Kelvindale. Maryhill's history, however, goes back to 1858 when the first Maryhill station opened. It was renamed Maryhill Central when Maryhill Barracks station opened. When reopened in 1993 it became simply Maryhill again.
See Chapter 4: New lines for passengers, Maryhill-Anniesland
Maryhill annual passenger numbers: 90,484

MATLOCK BATH Derbyshire   27 May 1972

On the single line from Ambergate to Matlock Town, the intermediate Matlock Bath

MARYHILL: An 1878 stained glass panel from Maryhill Burgh Halls shows a porter with a steam locomotive in the background. The 1858 station allowed prosperous residents from north west Glasgow to commute to work in central Glasgow

caters for the main tourist centre of this scenic valley. The platform was reopened following pressure from the local community. The station had closed in 1967. Matlock Bath annual passenger numbers: 70,588

MEADOWHALL South Yorkshire   05 Sep 1990

This new four-platform interchange station, north of Sheffield, serves a shopping and leisure complex. It has a 200-space car park. Sheffield Supertram also serves the station. Meadowhall annual passenger numbers: 2,138,462

MELKSHAM Wiltshire   13 May 1985

This station was reopened on an experimental basis for a new train service on the 16km Trowbridge-Chippenham line. The cost of £1,500 for a shelter and lighting was met by Melksham Town Council and Wiltshire County Council. The original station closed in 1966. In 2009 Wiltshire County Council bought the former goods yard on adjacent land from BRB (Residuary) Ltd in order to safeguard the site for improvements to the station access and facilities should there be an increase in the number of trains running through the station. Train services improved dramatically in December 2013, when train frequency increased from two each way per day to eight each way. Growth has exceeded all expectations.   Melksham annual passenger numbers: 60,676

MELTON Suffolk   03 Sep 1984

This station on the Ipswich-Lowestoft line reopened with funding from Suffolk County Council. It had been closed since 1955.   Melton annual passenger numbers: 63,510

MERRYTON South Lanarkshire   12 Dec 2005

One of two new intermediate single-platform stations, this is on the £35 million reopened Haughhead junction to Larkhall line, now served by electric trains from Glasgow. Merryton is listed as Merrytown by the Office of Rail Regulation and by National Rail Enquiries.   Merryton annual passenger numbers: 113,546

MERTHYR TYDFIL Merthyr Tudful   14 Jan 1996

The station was relocated to provide room for a retail development. The new station consists of a single terminal platform, recently extended, together with a waiting room and booking office. This is the third station site to be used in Merthyr for the terminus of the line from Cardiff. There is a bus link to Brecon from near the station. Merthyr Tydfil annual passenger numbers: 580,554

METHERINGHAM Lincolnshire   06 Oct 1975

Between Lincoln and Sleaford, this station was reopened at a cost of £7,415 met by Lincolnshire County Council. It has two platforms, shelters, lighting, fencing and a car park. In 2007 refurbishments and disability compliance measures costing £500,000, including rebuilt platforms with tactile paving, access ramps, new waiting shelters and improved lighting, were completed by Network Rail. Metheringham acts as a railhead for a large rural area.   Metheringham annual passenger numbers: 106,248

METROCENTRE Tyne and Wear   03 Aug 1987

The station was opened as Gateshead MetroCentre experimentally under the Speller legislation on the Newcastle-Carlisle line by a development company, which had built a vast shopping facility. In 1993 it was renamed MetroCentre. MetroCentre annual passenger numbers: 354,240

MILLIKEN PARK Renfrewshire   15 May 1989

On the Glasgow-Ayr line, this station south of Paisley was reopened at a cost of £240,000, funded by Strathclyde Regional Council. The previous station had closed in 1966.
Milliken Park annual passenger numbers: 206,100

MILLS HILL Greater Manchester   25 Mar 1985

Opened experimentally to serve Middleton on the Rochdale line, it used the same site as an earlier station which had closed in 1842.
Mills Hill annual passenger numbers: 310,032

MILTON KEYNES CENTRAL Buckinghamshire   15 May 1982

When the new town of Milton Keynes was planned in 1967 it was envisaged as a city of the car. It took 15 years before this five-platform station, which has a 600-space car park, was opened on the West Coast main line. The £3 million cost was met by British Rail and Milton Keynes Development Corporation. In 2005 the Government announced funding for a sixth (northbound) platform and to convert another platform into a through London-bound platform. The £200 million remodelling started in 2007 and was largely complete in summer 2008. It is hoped that services from Bedford will be extended from Bletchley to Milton Keynes Central.
Milton Keynes Central annual passenger numbers: 6,835,570

MITCHAM EASTFIELDS Greater London   03 Jun 2008

Picture: Ian McDonald

This £6 million two-platform station, which straddles Eastfields Road level crossing, has a ticket office, lifts and a footbridge. Located between Streatham and Mitcham junction and developed in partnership with Merton Council and Transport for London, it became the first new station in South London for more than 60 years. It was one of the first of a new generation of Network Rail modular stations, which was constructed off-site and lifted into place in sections, causing less disruption to services. It incorporates solar panels and rainwater harvesting to reduce utility bills.
Mitcham Eastfields annual passenger numbers: 1,538,936

MITCHAM EASTFIELDS: This £6 million station was one of the first of a new type of Network Rail modular designs, built off-site and lifted into place in sections

MOOR STREET
See entry under Birmingham Moor Street.

MOORFIELDS Merseyside   02 May 1977
Moorfields is an underground station, built partly as a replacement for Liverpool Exchange station. Twin platforms were built to serve the new tunnel linking the north and south suburban lines. A deep-level platform was also built on the single one-way clockwise loop for Wirral line trains. Moorfields annual passenger numbers: 6,996,347

MOSS SIDE Lancashire   21 Nov 1983
A single platform on the Blackpool South to Kirkham line was reopened here experimentally for £8,650, of which £7,000 came from Lancashire County Council. Moss Side annual passenger numbers: 2,284

MOSSPARK Glasgow   30 Jul 1990
One of five new stations on the Paisley Canal line, this station reopened at a cost of £101,000, funded by Strathclyde Regional Council. It had closed in 1983. Mosspark annual passenger numbers: 143,090

MOULSECOOMB East Sussex   15 May 1980
Opened for £244,000 funded by British Rail, this new station has twin platforms, a footbridge and station buildings which are served by Brighton-Eastbourne trains. East Sussex County Council contributed £6,500. Moulsecoomb annual passenger numbers: 422,406

MOUNT VERNON Glasgow   04 Oct 1993
One of five new stations provided as part of the Glasgow-Whifflet reopening of a freight-only line to passengers. Mount Vernon annual passenger numbers: 60,150

MOUNTAIN ASH Rhondda Cynon Taf   03 Oct 1988
ABERPENNAR

A single-platform station was provided in 1988 on the former freight line to Aberdare, but in 2001 a new two-platform station with a passing loop and ramped footbridge was built as a replacement on a deviated line. The original station had closed in 1964. Mountain Ash annual passenger numbers: 98,920

MUIR OF ORD Ross and Cromarty   04 Oct 1976
This station was reopened for trains on the Inverness-Dingwall line. Muir of Ord annual passenger numbers: 66,480

MUSSELBURGH East Lothian   03 Oct 1988

This station on the East Coast main line just east of Edinburgh was opened
experimentally as part of the Edinburgh to North Berwick electric service. The £366,000
cost was funded by Lothian Regional Council. Since 2009 the station has served the
new Queen Margaret University.
Musselburgh annual passenger numbers: 478,100

NARBOROUGH Leicestershire   05 Jan 1970

This station on the Leicester-Nuneaton line was reopened soon after closure in March
1968. The cost of £3,250 for general restoration was met by Blaby Rural District Council
and Blaby Parish Council.
Narborough annual passenger numbers: 386,782

NEEDHAM MARKET Suffolk   06 Dec 1971

This fine station on the Norwich-Ipswich line reopened with funds from Gipping Rural
District Council. In 2000, the station building was restored and won a National Railway
Heritage award two years later. The station had closed in 1967.
Needham Market annual passenger numbers: 88,242

NEWBRIDGE Caerphilly   06 Feb 2008
TRECELYN *Caerffili*

One of six new stations on the Ebbw Valley line, this single-platform station is on the
site of a former station which closed in 1962.
See Chapter 4: New lines for passengers, Ebbw Valley line
Newbridge annual passenger numbers: 127,100

NEWBURY RACECOURSE Berkshire   16 May 1988

This station, on the Reading-Newbury main line, and used occasionally for horse racing
events, was reopened for regular services following local housing development.
Newbury Racecourse annual passenger numbers: 97,254

NEW CUMNOCK East Ayrshire   27 May 1991

This station reopened on the Glasgow-Dumfries line at a cost of £410,000, funded by
Strathclyde Regional Council. It has two platforms, shelters, a long ramped access, car

73

park and long-line public address system. The original had closed in 1965.
New Cumnock annual passenger numbers: 28,416

NEW HOLLAND Lincolnshire   24 Jun 1981

This £20,000 station was funded by Humberside County Council to replace the New
Holland Town station, which became redundant with the withdrawal of ferry services
after the opening of the new Humber Road Bridge. The station is on the Barton-
Cleethorpes line.
New Holland annual passenger numbers: 14,708

NEW PUDSEY West Yorkshire   06 Mar 1967

This new station between Bradford and Leeds was funded by British Rail and was an
early parkway-style station. It replaced Stanningley, one kilometre away, which closed
in December 1967.
New Pudsey annual passenger numbers: 891,062

NEWCOURT Devon   4 Jun 2015

Newcourt was the first new rail station in Devon for 20 years, apart from Sampford
Courtney on the preserved Dartmoor Railway. Newcourt serves a new housing
development on the site of a former Royal Navy stores depot. Newcourt station is on
the Exmouth line, close to Exeter Chiefs rugby ground at Sandy Park. More housing and
an Ikea furniture store are also planned. The £2.2 million Newcourt station is part of the
county council's Metro plan to create an alternative to car use and received £741,000

Picture: Rob Cousins

**NEWCOURT: An Exmouth train passes by in January 2015 as the new station slowly
takes shape. The platform supports can be seen in place**

funding from the Department for Transport's new station fund. Two more stations are also planned.
Newcourt annual passenger numbers: 59,410

NEWCRAIGHALL Edinburgh   03 Jun 2002

Located south of Portobello on the Millerhill freight branch, this 300-metre single-platform station includes a 586-space car park for passengers using Edinburgh Crossrail services. Trackwork, signalling, and the two new stations incurred an overall cost of £8 million. The service improved dramatically when the Borders Railway reopened in 2015.
Newcraighall annual passenger numbers: 224,026

NEWSTEAD Nottinghamshire   08 May 1993

This £2.7 million station with a single platform opened as the temporary terminus for the 17km Phase 1 of the Robin Hood line from Nottingham. Since March 2004 it has offered connections to Nottingham Express trams.
Newstead annual passenger numbers: 31,932

NEWTON AYCLIFFE Durham   01 Jan 1978

This new station on the route of the original Stockton-Darlington Railway opened to serve the new town.
Newton Aycliffe annual passenger numbers: 60,548

NEWTONGRANGE Midlothian   6 Sep 2015

Newtongrange station was one of seven new stations on the reopened Borders Railway from Edinburgh Waverley to Tweedbank. The single-platform Newtongrange is a few hundred metres from the earlier station site and provides a direct link to Scotland's National Mining Museum at the former Lady Victoria Colliery.
See Chapter 4: New lines for passengers, Edinburgh-Tweedbank
Newtongrange annual passenger numbers: 86,398

NINIAN PARK Cardiff   04 Oct 1987
PARC NINIAN Caerdydd

The reconstruction of this twin-platform station, which reopened experimentally at a cost of £60,000, was funded by South Glamorgan County Council. It is served by the new Cardiff City line.
Ninian Park annual passenger numbers: 105,784

OKEHAMPTON Devon   **25 May 1997**

Following purchase of the 29km Crediton-Okehampton branch line by the Camas Quarry Company, Devon County Council acquired and renovated Okehampton station and sponsored six return trains to and from Exeter on summer Sundays, starting in 1997. This service continues to offer successful Dartmoor explorer opportunities and there is a local campaign to re-establish a permanent service. Reopening Exeter-Okehampton-Plymouth was mooted as part of the South West Resilience proposals in 2015 and in May 2017 Transport Secretary Chris Grayling was said to be working with rail bosses on a trial commuter service from Okehampton to Exeter. As a way of demonstrating the potential, OkeRail campaigners organised the Royal Oke train from Okehampton to London Paddington in March 2017. The journey was planned by voluntary groups, Okerail Forum and Okerail community interest company, with the undertaking underwritten by Okehampton United Charity. 500 tickets were sold out in four days. The original station had closed in 1972.
Okehampton annual passenger numbers: 3,036

Picture: OkeRail

OKEHAMPTON CAMPAIGNERS AT PADDINGTON 2017: Okehampton station is there but the campaign goes on to obtain a good service

OUTWOOD West Yorkshire   12 Jul 1988

This £170,000 station on the Wakefield-Leeds line is near the former Lofthouse station that had closed in 1960.
Outwood annual passenger numbers: 390,490

OVERPOOL Cheshire   16 Aug 1988

This station on the Ellesmere-Hooton line has twin six-car platforms costing £263,000. Most of the cost was funded by £193,000 from Cheshire County Council, and the balance came from Merseyside Passenger Transport Executive.
Overpool annual passenger numbers: 159,166

OXFORD PARKWAY Oxfordshire   26 Oct 2015

Prime Minister David Cameron made a guest appearance when Oxford Parkway station (provisionally named Water Eaton Parkway) opened in North Oxford as part of Chiltern Railways' plan to provide a route to Oxford from London Marylebone. The station was built next to the Water Eaton park-and-ride site. Legal challenges delayed the rail plan and the line from Oxford Parkway into the main Oxford station opened more than a year later on 11 December 2016. The parkway station has two nine-car platforms and more than 800 car parking places in addition to the adjoining park-and-ride bus station. There are also 150 bike parking spaces. The station is on national cycle route 51.
See Chapter 4: New lines for passengers, Oxford Parkway-Oxford
Oxford Parkway annual passenger numbers: 274,696

Picture: Ray King

OXFORD PARKWAY: Chiltern Railways reached the outskirts of Oxford from London Marylebone with the opening of Oxford Parkway

P

PAISLEY CANAL Renfrewshire   30 Jul 1990

This was one of five new stations on the Paisley Canal line which formerly ran to Kilmacolm but was closed in 1983. Part of the route was retained for freight use but the route was quickly built over west of Paisley Canal station. The station itself cost £193,000, funded by Strathclyde Regional Council and is a single-line terminus served by half-hourly diesel multiple units from Glasgow.
Paisley Canal annual passenger numbers: 367,690

PARTICK Glasgow   05 Nov 1979
PARTAIG

Partick station is a combined railway and underground station. It was formed through the amalgamation of Partickhill station and the Merkland Street underground station on a single site. It is one of the primary stations on the Argyle line and North Clyde line of Strathclyde Partnership for Transport's suburban rail network. These lines mainly provide services to the east and west although the station itself is orientated north-south with two platforms.   Partick annual passenger numbers: 2,857,994

PEARTREE Derbyshire   04 Oct 1976

This local station 2km south of Derby, formerly Peartree and Normanton until it closed in 1968, reopened to serve workers of a Rolls-Royce factory, but sadly now has a very infrequent service. A press release from the Association of Train Operators in 2008 wrongly claimed that it had been closed.   Peartree annual passenger numbers: 5,022

PENALLY Pembrokeshire *Sir Benfro*   28 Feb 1972

This single-platform reopened station is just west of Tenby on the Whitland-Pembroke line. The original station had closed in 1964 but reopened temporarily in the summer only in 1970 and 1971.   Penally annual passenger numbers: 5,444

PENCOED Bridgend *Pen-y-bont ar Ogwr*   11 May 1992

On the Cardiff-Bridgend main line, this station reopened with new four-car platforms staggered on either side of the town's level crossing.
Pencoed annual passenger numbers: 236,902

PENRHIWCEIBER Rhondda Cynon Taf   03 Oct 1988

This two-car platform, subsequently extended to accommodate four cars, is one of six stations on the Abercynon-Aberdare line. An earlier station had closed for regular passenger use in 1964 but survived as an excursion station for some time. Penrhiwceiber annual passenger numbers: 48,784

PINHOE Devon   16 May 1983

Reopened for a three-year experiment, this station was the first under the Speller legislation (see notes at end of this chapter), and is 5km east of Exeter on the Salisbury line. Devon County Council contributed £5,000. The original station had closed in 1966. Pinhoe annual passenger numbers: 94,354

PONTEFRACT TANSHELF West Yorkshire   11 May 1992

Opened as one of three new stations on the 13km former freight-only route linking Wakefield and Pontefract, it cost £1.1 million funded by West Yorkshire Passenger Transport Authority and a European Regional Development Fund grant. The original Tanshelf station closed in 1967. Pontefract Tanshelf annual passenger numbers: 32,508

PONTYCLUN *Rhondda Cynon Taf*   28 Sep 1992

Opened on the South Wales main line east of Bridgend, this two-platform station on the South Wales main line is on the site of the former Llantrisant station. The new station is mainly served by trains to Maesteg. Pontyclun annual passenger numbers: 301,474

PORTLETHEN Aberdeenshire   17 May 1985

After being closed for nearly 30 years, this station on the Aberdeen-Stonehaven line opened experimentally again at a cost of £120,000, which was met by Grampian Regional Council.   Portlethen annual passenger numbers: 56,324

POSSILPARK & PARKHOUSE Glasgow   03 Dec 1993

This station reopened on the Glasgow to Maryhill north suburban line, funded by Strathclyde Regional Council, on the site of the former station which had closed to advertised services in 1917. Possilpark & Parkhouse annual passenger numbers: 91,392

PRESTWICK INTERNATIONAL AIRPORT Ayrshire   05 Sep 1994

This new station opened on the electrified Glasgow-Ayr line to serve Prestwick Airport. The station, which is 46km from Glasgow Central, was funded by the airport operators PIK Holdings, Enterprise Ayrshire, Kyle and Carrick District Council and Strathclyde Regional Council. The two-platform station has lifts and escalators to a covered walkway giving direct access to the airport terminal building. The airport operators, in co-operation with ScotRail and the airlines, organised a through ticketing scheme.

Although estimates had suggested only negligible use of such an adjacent rail station, Prestwick International Airport Rail station was carrying over 30% of all surface arrival and departure passengers for the airport by 2010.
Prestwick International Airport annual passenger numbers: 392,858

PRIESTHILL & DARNLEY Glasgow   23 Apr 1990

This station on the Glasgow-Kilmarnock line opened at a cost of £291,000, funded by Strathclyde Regional Council. Sunday trains providing an hourly service to Glasgow Central were introduced in May 2017 for the first time.
Priesthill & Darnley annual passenger numbers: 137,668

PYE CORNER Newport   14 Dec 2014

The £3.5 million Pye Corner station was opened in 2014 in the residential Rogerstone area of Newport as part of the project to allow Ebbw Vale line trains to serve Newport as well as Cardiff. Opening the station was a priority in the 2008 regional transport plan of the South East Wales Transport Alliance. The new single-platform station is close to the former Bassaleg Junction station and was jointly funded by the Welsh Government and the Department for Transport.
Pye Corner annual passenger numbers: 63,332

PYLE Bridgend   27 Jun 1994
Y PIL Pen-y-bont ar Ogwr

This station is located between Port Talbot and Bridgend on the South Wales main line. It is the third station site to be used at Pyle.
Pyle annual passenger numbers: 120,732

NATIONAL RAIL USE: Statistics from the Office of Rail and Road

RAMSGREAVE & WILPSHIRE Lancashire **29 May 1994**

This new station is 4km from the Blackburn end of the Ribble Valley line, one of three which reopened at the same time as the line to Clitheroe reopened to regular passenger trains in 1994. The original Wilpshire station had closed in 1962.
Ramsgreave & Wilpshire annual passenger numbers: 96,832

RAMSLINE HALT Derbyshire **20 Jan 1990**

This was designed for use by football specials bringing fans to Derby County Football Club's adjoining Baseball Ground. The single platform, alongside a through siding, opened after contributions from Derbyshire County Council, the Football Trust, Derby County FC, the Government and British Rail. The station is no longer in use as Derby County FC moved to Pride Park Stadium in 1997.

RHOOSE CARDIFF INTERNATIONAL AIRPORT **12 Jun 2005**
Vale of Glamorgan

MAES AWYR RHYNGWLADOL CAERDYDD Y RHWS
Bro Morgannwg

The station on the reopened Vale of Glamorgan route serves the nearby Cardiff International Airport via a free seven-minute long shuttle bus link. The station opened along with Llantwit Major as part of a £13 million scheme to restore passenger services over the coastal route between Cardiff and Bridgend. Rhoose station had closed in 1964.
Rhoose Cardiff International Airport annual passenger numbers: 182,750

RIBBLEHEAD North Yorkshire **1986**

Ribblehead railway station is at the south end of Ribblehead viaduct. It was reopened in 1986 by British Rail with one southbound platform. A second platform was opened in 1993. The station is leased by the Settle and Carlisle Railway Trust which has restored it and provided a visitor centre.
Ribblehead annual passenger numbers: 18,930

RISCA & PONTYMISTER Caerphilly **06 Feb 2008**
RHISGA A PHONT-Y-MEISTR *Caerffili*

One of six new stations on the Ebbw Valley line, this two-platform station opened when

81

services between Cardiff Central and Ebbw Vale Parkway began.
See Chapter 4: New lines for passengers, Ebbw Valley line
Risca & Pontymister annual passenger numbers: 100,960

ROGART Lairg   06 Mar 1961

This two-platform station on the Lairg Loop section of the Far North line reopened less than nine months after it closed in 1960.   Rogart annual passenger numbers: 1,710

ROGERSTONE Newport   06 Feb 2008
Y TŶ-DU   Casnewydd

This single-platform station is one of six new stations on the Ebbw Valley line and is within a district of the city of Newport.
See Chapter 4: New lines for passengers, Ebbw Valley line
Rogerstone annual passenger numbers: 85,658

ROTHERHAM CENTRAL South Yorkshire   11 May 1987

Trains between Sheffield and Doncaster gain access to this station using a new 0.5km single track link, known as the Holmes chord. The overall cost of £2.4 million was met by South Yorkshire Passenger Transport Executive with the benefit of a 50% European Regional Development Fund grant and a contribution from Rotherham District Council.
Rotherham Central annual passenger numbers: 689,540

ROUGHTON ROAD Norfolk   20 May 1985

Just south of Cromer, this £62,000 single-platform station was opened for Norwich-Sheringham Bittern line trains. British Rail met £11,000 of the cost, North Norfolk District Council paid £7,000 and the Manpower Services Commission paid £44,000. It was the culmination of a nine-year local campaign.
Roughton Road annual passenger numbers: 12,814

RUGELEY TOWN Staffordshire   01 Jun 1997

This new twin-platform station close to Rugeley town centre and new housing estates was reopened eight years after the earlier Chase line reopening had reached Hednesford. Waiting shelters, a footbridge and adjacent car park were included. The cost of nearly £1 million was met by Staffordshire County Council and Cannock Chase District Council. Trains now run through to Birmingham. The original station closed in 1965.   Rugeley Town annual passenger numbers: 140,838

RUNCORN EAST Cheshire   03 Oct 1983

This new station provided rail services on the Warrington-Chester line for new housing estates. It has twin platforms for eight cars, a ticket office, waiting shelters, car parking,

lighting and a ramped footbridge. The £385,000 cost was met by contributions of £100,000 each from Warrington Development Corporation and Cheshire County Council, and the balance was covered by British Rail. A 30% grant was also received from the European Community.
Runcorn East annual passenger numbers: 183,930

RUSKINGTON Lincolnshire   05 May 1975

On the Lincoln-Sleaford line, this station reopened for just £8,523, paid for by Lincolnshire County Council. The twin platforms have shelters, lighting and a car park. The original station had closed in 1961.
Ruskington annual passenger numbers: 87,328

RUTHERGLEN South Lanarkshire   05 Nov 1979

The station was relocated to be served by Argyle line trains when local services were transferred from Glasgow Central high level to the low-level Argyle line.
Rutherglen annual passenger numbers: 1,110,088

RYDER BROW Greater Manchester   04 Nov 1985

This station opened experimentally to serve the Ryder Brow area of Gorton in Manchester and was funded by the Greater Manchester Passenger Transport Executive.
Ryder Brow annual passenger numbers: 27,078

ST MICHAELS Liverpool   03 Jan 1978

This station, which had closed in 1972, reopened six years later along with Aigburth on the Liverpool Northern line, and was well used for the International Garden Festival in 1984.
St Michaels annual passenger numbers: 977,510

ST PANCRAS

See London St Pancras.

ST PAUL'S THAMESLINK

See City Thameslink.

SALFORD CRESCENT Greater Manchester   **11 May 1987**

At the northern end of the new Windsor Link line, this new island station opened at
a cost of £660,000 met jointly by British Rail and Greater Manchester Passenger
Transport Executive.
Salford Crescent annual passenger numbers: 955,878

SALTAIRE West Yorkshire   **10 Apr 1984**

Using the site of a station closed in March 1965, this £139,000 station opening
was funded by the West Yorkshire Passenger Transport Executive with a European
Community grant. It is situated near Shipley on the Skipton to Bradford and Leeds line.
Saltaire annual passenger numbers: 880,348

SAMPFORD COURTENAY Devon   **21 May 2004**

Although sited on the now privately owned Crediton-Okehampton branch line, the
Dartmoor Railway Company reopened this single platform station for the summer
services sponsored by Devon County Council. The original station had closed in 1972.
Sampford Courtenay annual passenger numbers: 130

SANDAL & AGBRIGG West Yorkshire   **30 Nov 1987**

This £180,000 station is south of Wakefield on the Doncaster line. Since May 1988 it has
also been served by Leeds-Sheffield trains.
Sandal & Agbrigg annual passenger numbers: 274,996

Picture: Ray King

SANQUHAR: There is a train approximately every two hours to both Glasgow and
Dumfries during the week but the Sunday service is hopelessly inadequate

SANDWELL & DUDLEY West Midlands   1984

An earlier Oldbury station was rebuilt and reopened in 1984 as Sandwell and Dudley
with longer platforms capable of handling inter-city trains.
Sandwell & Dudley annual passenger numbers: 908,982

SANQUHAR Dumfries and Galloway   27 Jun 1994

This station on the Nith Valley line (Glasgow-Dumfries-Carlisle) opened at a cost of
£375,000, funded by Dumfries and Galloway Enterprise. The original had closed in 1965.
Sanquhar annual passenger numbers: 24,532

SARN Bridgend *Pen-y-bont ar Ogwr*   28 Sep 1992

This station is just 3km north of Bridgend and is one of six new stations opened for
Cardiff-Maesteg services.   Sarn annual passenger numbers: 62,970

SHAWFAIR Midlothian   6 Sep 2015

Shawfair station was one of seven new stations on the reopened Borders Railway
from Edinburgh Waverley to Tweedbank. The double platform station serves a new
development which did not exist when the original Waverley line was closed.
See Chapter 4: New lines for passengers, Edinburgh-Tweedbank
Shawfair annual passenger numbers: 13,202

SHEPHERD'S BUSH Greater London   28 Sep 2008

This new station on London Overground's West London line between Willesden
Junction and Kensington Olympia is near to Shepherd's Bush on London
Underground's Central line. It was designed and funded by the developers of Westfield
Shopping Centre and aimed to cope with up to 70,000 commuters a week. In 2015 the

Picture: Ian McDonald

SHEPHERD'S BUSH: The new station is very popular with shoppers

platforms were doubled in length to allow for eight-car trains. Construction started in early 2006 and was completed according to the original design in 2007. However, at a late stage it was discovered that almost the entire length of the northern platform was up to 45 centimetres too narrow, with barely enough space to walk round the lamp posts without crossing the yellow line. Changes had to be made before opening. The station includes a ticket office, lifts and CCTV. The Westfield developers also funded nearby Wood Lane station on the Hammersmith & City line – the first new London Underground station on an existing line for more than 70 years – which opened on 14 Oct 2008.   Shepherd's Bush annual passenger numbers: 8,653,428

SHERBURN-IN-ELMET North Yorkshire   09 Jul 1984

After being closed for 19 years, this station on the York-Pontefract line reopened experimentally for six months following a grant from Selby District Council. As the patronage was satisfactory, the station has remained open.
Sherburn-in-Elmet annual passenger numbers: 50,132

SHIELDMUIR North Lanarkshire   14 May 1990

Opened at a cost of £288,000, this two-platform station uses an existing footbridge and land from former sidings, and was funded by Strathclyde Regional Council. Just south of Motherwell on the electrified West Coast main line, it is served by the hourly Lanark service. Much of the area was derelict and the initial patronage was disappointing but usage doubled in 2008.   Shieldmuir annual passenger numbers: 105,166

SHIREBROOK Derbyshire   24 May 1998

North of Mansfield Woodhouse, this is one of four additional stations forming the Robin Hood Phase 3 extension to Worksop. Shirebrook opened at a cost of £5 million, with contributions from the European Regional Development Fund, Capital Challenge, Single Regeneration Budget and Railtrack. The original station closed in 1964.
See Chapter 4: New lines for passengers, Robin Hood line
Shirebrook annual passenger numbers: 87,276

SHOREDITCH HIGH STREET Greater London   27 Apr 2010

Shoreditch High Street is a completely new station built as part of the London Overground's East London line project. It replaced Shoreditch station which was the terminus of the East London line until 2006. The new station was built on the site of Bishopsgate goods station which was destroyed by fire in 1964.
See Chapter 4: New lines for passengers, East London line
Shoreditch High Street annual passenger numbers: 7,661,254

SHOTTON Low Level Flintshire *Sir y Fflint*   21 Aug 1972

Situated on the North Wales coast line, the Low Level station reopened six years after it was closed by British Rail. Since then it has afforded an interchange with the High Level platforms on the Wrexham-Liverpool line. Shotton annual passenger numbers: 237,194

SILEBY Leicestershire   27 May 1994

On the site of the original station which closed in 1968, on the Midland main line, Sileby has two platforms. It was one of three stations opened as Phase 1 of the Ivanhoe line project.
Sileby annual passenger numbers: 123,694

SILKSTONE COMMON South Yorkshire   26 Nov 1984

With £60,000 funding from South Yorkshire Passenger Transport Executive, this station on the Huddersfield-Denby Dale-Sheffield line was reopened, 25 years after an earlier station had closed.
Silkstone Common annual passenger numbers: 39,488

SINFIN CENTRAL Derbyshire   04 Oct 1976
SINFIN NORTH Derbyshire   04 Oct 1976

These new three-car single-platform stations, on a 1.5km branch south of Derby, opened following expenditure by Derbyshire County Council. The catchment was exclusively confined to an industrial area (several Rolls-Royce factory sites close to Sinfin Central) and thus patronage was limited to peak-hour traffic, with only two trains per day, running to and from Matlock, reduced to just one in 1992.
With no access for the general public, and the refusal by Rolls-Royce to allow employees to adjust their working hours to suit the train times, usage was inevitably minimal, and on 17 May 1993 (when the Derwent Valley line, which connected with the Sinfin branch, switched to Sprinter Units that could not run on the line because of signalling limitations) the service ceased and taxis were substituted. Formal closure notices for both stations were issued in December 1997. Consent to close the stations was given by the Office of the Rail Regulator in May 1998. The line has remained open for freight.

SKEWEN Neath Port Talbot   27 Jun 1994
SGIWEN Castell-nedd Port Talbot

West of Neath, this station reopened for Swanline services operating between Cardiff and Swansea, 30 years after the original station closed.
Skewen annual passenger numbers: 45,172

SLAITHWAITE West Yorkshire   13 Dec 1982

Opened in Huddersfield on the site of the station closed in October 1968, Slaithwaite station was funded by West Yorkshire Passenger Transport Executive with £120,000.
Slaithwaite annual passenger numbers: 212,608

SMALLBROOK JUNCTION Isle of Wight   20 Jul 1991

This station opened on the singled Island line specifically to provide cross-platform interchange with the Isle of Wight Steam Railway. Trains stop there only when the steam service is running.
Smallbrook Junction annual passenger numbers: 12,134

SMETHWICK GALTON BRIDGE West Midlands   24 Sep 1995

This two-level station has replaced Smethwick West. It was built on a viaduct over a canal and alongside a steep embankment – hence the £3.9 million cost – to provide an interchange between the Snow Hill and New Street lines, as well as serving urban housing and industry.
Smethwick Galton Bridge annual passenger numbers: 639,594

SMITHY BRIDGE Greater Manchester   18 Aug 1985

Funded by Greater Manchester Passenger Transport Executive, this station reopened experimentally to serve a small community north of Rochdale with Halifax to Manchester Victoria trains, 25 years after the original station had closed.
Smithy Bridge annual passenger numbers: 149,152

SNOW HILL Birmingham

See Birmingham Snow Hill.

SOUTH BANK Redcar and Cleveland   01 Jul 1984

Re-sited in 1984 because of a road scheme funded by Cleveland County Council and the then Department of Transport, this station is situated on the Middlesbrough-Saltburn line.
South Bank annual passenger numbers: 21,846

SOUTH GYLE Edinburgh   01 May 1985

Opened experimentally on the Edinburgh to Fife line, at a cost of £226,290 funded by Lothian Regional Council, this station serves a large area of the western side of Edinburgh as a park-and-ride station, and also serves a rapidly developing commercial and industrial area. In its first year it handled 4,000 passengers per week, and has since continued to expand.
South Gyle annual passenger numbers: 587,432

SOUTH WIGSTON Leicestershire   10 May 1986

This station, 6km south of Leicester on the Nuneaton-Leicester line, opened at a cost of £135,000 to Leicestershire County Council. Patronage has been 50% greater than forecast and extra services have been provided. The station has staggered platforms and serves a large housing estate. Wigston Glen Parva station had closed in 1968. South Wigston annual passenger numbers: 74,858

SOUTHAMPTON AIRPORT PARKWAY Hampshire   01 Apr 1966

Opened as Southampton Airport, this station was further developed and reopened as Southampton Parkway in 1986 to serve the adjacent airport and for use as a commuter station for the nearby M27 motorway. In 2009 £2.9 million (including £600,00 from BAA and £90,000 from Hampshire County Council) was spent on improvements. Two new platform lifts and a new footbridge, which is located close to the arrivals hall in the airport terminal, were built as part of the Government's Access for All scheme. Southampton Airport Parkway annual passenger numbers: 1,819,432

SOUTHBURY Greater London   21 Nov 1960

This station was opened on the Southbury Loop in conjunction with the electrification of the line from Liverpool Street to Seven Sisters and Cheshunt. The original station on the site, called Churchbury, closed in 1909.
Southbury annual passenger numbers: 833,988

SOUTHEND AIRPORT Essex   18 Jul 2011

Planning permission for this station was granted by Rochford District Council in 1997 but it was not until 2011 that the Stobart Group, which bought Southend Airport in 2008, opened this £12 million station providing a direct service to London. The station was officially opened by the then transport minister Theresa Villiers in September 2011. A new terminal building adjoining the station opened in 2012. In 2017, the airport is served by easyJet and Flybe. Passengers requiring the airport previously had to alight at Rochford station and then take a bus or taxi to the airport. Staff at the station are employed by Stobart.   Southend Airport annual passenger numbers: 425,160

STANSTED AIRPORT Essex   19 Mar 1991

A £44 million 5.5km new rail link was built to connect the Liverpool Street-Cambridge line with the airport terminal via a triangular junction and an electrified single line to a three-platform station. Sensibly an edge for a fourth platform was also constructed. Unfortunately, only a single-bore tunnel was constructed under the runway, placing a limit of seven paths an hour on the line. There are four trains each hour to London, one an hour to Birmingham via Cambridge, and a local service to Stratford started in December 2005. The latest proposal is to extend the third platform to accommodate four-car trains, and to open up the fourth platform.
Stansted Airport annual passenger numbers: 6,012,526

STEETON & SILSDEN West Yorkshire   14 May 1990

Built on the site of the former platforms, this £260,000 station opened on the Keighley-

Skipton-Bradford line. The earlier station had closed in 1965.
Steeton & Silsden annual passenger numbers: 838,874

STEPPS North Lanarkshire   15 May 1989

Reopened on the Glasgow-Springburn-Cumbernauld line, this station cost
£291,000 and was funded by Strathclyde Regional Council. The original station had
closed in 1962. Stepps annual passenger numbers: 300,424

STEVENAGE Hertfordshire   23 Jul 1973

Relocated as an inter-city parkway station 1.6km south of the old station on the East
Coast main line and nearer the centre of town, this station, with four 12-car island
platforms, is served by local trains and some express services.
Stevenage annual passenger numbers: 4,759,972

STEWARTON East Ayrshire   05 Jun 1967

On the Glasgow to Kilmarnock line, this station was reopened with one platform, less
than a year after being closed. A second platform was added in 2008 after the track was
doubled between Stewarton and Lugton.
Stewarton annual passenger numbers: 321,706

STOW Midlothian   6 Sep 2015

Stow station was one of seven new stations on the reopened Borders Railway from
Edinburgh Waverley to Tweedbank. The new Stow (pronounced to rhyme with how)
station has two platforms and is on the site of the old station.
See Chapter 4: New lines for passengers, Edinburgh-Tweedbank
Stow annual passenger numbers: 39,656

STRATFORD INTERNATIONAL Greater London   30 Nov 2009

Billed as East London's gateway to Paris and Brussels, this £30 million station on Britain's
High Speed 1 rail line was completed as early as 2006 and serves the 2012 Olympic
Games site and the new Westfield shopping centre. It is served by domestic high-
speed services from St Pancras International to Kent, and in 2010, an extension of the
Docklands Light Railway connected the new station to the existing regional station at
Stratford, half a kilometre away. Local politicians had hoped that Eurostar trains would
stop at Stratford International but so far that has not happened.
Stratford International annual passenger numbers: 1,632,646

STRATFORD-upon-AVON PARKWAY Warwickshire 19 May 2013

Warwickshire County Council's cabinet approved preliminary plans for a new
£6.57 million station at Bishopton between Wilmcote and Stratford in 2009. Studies
indicated a benefit to cost ratio of 2.8:1, with 140,000 passengers a year predicted.

STRATFORD INTERNATIONAL: This picture shows the completed station in 2009. The station building straddles the tracks, sandwiched between the new multi-storey shopping centre (top right) and the DLR station under construction on the left

The station site is next to the existing park-and-ride facility, allowing it to share the 725-space car park.
Stratford Parkway annual passenger numbers: 83,228

STREETHOUSE West Yorkshire   11 May 1992

Opened on the former freight-only Wakefield-Pontefract line, it is 6km east of Wakefield Kirkgate station.
Streethouse annual passenger numbers: 27,870

SUGAR LOAF Powys   21 Jun 1987

Reopened experimentally on summer Sundays, this station on the Heart of Wales line is popular with ramblers. It appeared in the national timetable book in 1992, and since 1995 has been open seven days a week. It is a permanent request stop. It was sponsored by the Sports Council for Wales.
Sugar Loaf annual passenger numbers: 132

SUMMERSTON Glasgow   03 Dec 1993

This station on the Glasgow north suburban line to Maryhill was funded by Strathclyde Regional Council.
Summerston annual passenger numbers: 152,434

SUTTON PARKWAY Nottinghamshire   20 Nov 1995

This station with twin 79-metre platforms on the Robin Hood line has a large car parking area adjacent. The £650,000 project was funded by Ashfield District Council and lies on the eastern fringe of the town of Sutton-in-Ashfield.
Sutton Parkway annual passenger numbers: 180,510

SWINTON South Yorkshire   14 May 1990

The new three-platform Swinton station was provided as part of a £33 million scheme to rationalise tracks north of Rotherham and construct a new junction north of Swinton station. Swinton Town station had closed in 1968.
Swinton annual passenger numbers: 390,730

SYSTON Leicestershire   27 May 1994

This single-platform station is one of three stations opened as Phase 1 of the Ivanhoe line project. It is on the Midland main line, south of Syston junction, on a bi-directional slow line. Ample car parking is available nearby. The original station had closed in 1968.
Syston annual passenger numbers: 210,904

T

TAME BRIDGE PARKWAY West Midlands   04 Jun 1990

This new station was opened at the south end of the Bescot freight yards on the Birmingham New Street to Walsall line, at a cost of £600,000.
Tame Bridge Parkway annual passenger numbers: 578,164

TEES-SIDE AIRPORT Darlington   03 Oct 1971

Opened by British Rail, on the Darlington-Middlesbrough line, this serves the airport now known as Durham Tees Valley. Unfortunately this station sees only two trains each week, partly because it is at the opposite end of the airport to the terminal buildings.
Tees-side Airport annual passenger numbers: 98

TELFORD CENTRAL Shropshire   12 May 1986

This new station on the Wolverhampton-Shrewsbury line was built with two platforms long enough to accommodate inter-city through trains to Euston. It has a large car park and is surrounded by roads and the nearby M54, and so affords a parkway railhead for a wide area of Shropshire. The station cost £700,000 and was funded jointly by British Rail, Telford Development Corporation and Shropshire County Council.
Telford Central annual passenger numbers: 1,139,070

TEMPLECOMBE Somerset   03 Oct 1983

The reopening of Templecombe, on the Salisbury to Yeovil and Exeter main line, resulted from a local campaign. A contribution of £9,200 from Somerset County Council enabled British Rail to reopen this station, initially as an experiment. It had closed originally in 1966.
Templecombe annual passenger numbers: 115,378

THE HAWTHORNS West Midlands   24 Sep 1995

This £1.6 million station in Sandwell is close to The Hawthorns stadium, West Bromwich Albion's football ground. A 190-space car park is provided, and an adjacent interchange with Midland Metro is available.
The Hawthorns annual passenger numbers: 439,912

THEOBALDS GROVE Hertfordshire   21 Nov 1960

This station reopened on the Southbury loop and serves Waltham Cross. The line

regained full passenger services in 1960 when the routes to Bishops Stortford and Hertford were electrified.
Theobalds Grove annual passenger numbers: 351,986

THURNSCOE South Yorkshire   16 May 1988

This station on the Pontefract-Sheffield line opened following £180,000 expenditure by South Yorkshire Passenger Transport Executive, helped by a 50% grant from the European Community.
Thurnscoe annual passenger numbers: 77,528

TIVERTON PARKWAY Devon   12 May 1986

This new station, 1km north of the former Tiverton Junction, is next to junction 27 of the M5 motorway. It has 250 car parking spaces and was opened with inter-city length platforms and a colourful brick construction. The cost of £730,000 was principally met by British Rail, with contributions of £80,000 from Devon County Council, £50,000 from Mid Devon District Council and £30,000 worth of road improvements by Devon County Council.
Tiverton Parkway annual passenger numbers: 478,250

TONDU Bridgend *Pen-y-bont ar Ogwr*   28 Sep 1992

This is one of six new stations opened for Cardiff-Maesteg services. One platform at this former junction station on the Maesteg line was refurbished and reopened. The original station had closed in 1970.
Tondu annual passenger numbers: 41,222

TURKEY STREET Greater London   21 Nov 1960

This station on the Southbury loop of the Liverpool Street to Cheshunt line reopened when the line to Bishops Stortford and Hertford was electrified. It was rebuilt in the late 1980s. The original station on the site, called Forty Hill, closed in 1909.
Turkey Street annual passenger numbers: 603,754

TUTBURY AND HATTON Derbyshire   03 Apr 1989

This £79,000 station on the Stoke-Uttoxeter-Derby line opened on the site of the former Tutbury station, with contributions from eight authorities including Derbyshire and Staffordshire county councils. The two platforms are staggered on either side of a level crossing. Tutbury station had closed in 1966.
Tutbury and Hatton annual passenger numbers: 64,306

TWEEDBANK Selkirkshire   6 Sep 2015

Tweedbank station was one of seven new stations on the reopened Borders Railway

from Edinburgh Waverley to Tweedbank. The station uses a central platform with a line on either side. A station did not exist here when the Waverley line was closed.
See Chapter 4: New lines for passengers, Edinburgh-Tweedbank
Tweedbank annual passenger numbers: 300,602

TY GLAS Cardiff *Caerdydd*   29 Apr 1987

This two-car platform opened experimentally to serve housing, business and industrial areas on the Coryton branch line north of Cardiff. The cost of £78,000 was funded by South Glamorgan County Council.
Ty Glas annual passenger numbers: 180,420

U

UNIVERSITY West Midlands   08 May 1978

One of three new stations provided on the west suburban line, the twin six-car platforms on a severe curve cost £300,000 with stairs, footbridge and ticket office, and was funded by the West Midlands Passenger Transport Executive. Opened on a completely new site, the station serves the Birmingham University campus and the Queen Elizabeth Hospital complex.
University annual passenger numbers: 3,205,520

UPHALL West Lothian   24 Mar 1986

This station opened experimentally as part of the Bathgate line reopening, with funding from Lothian Regional Council, West Lothian District Council, the European Regional Development Fund and Livingston Development Corporation. At this time the line was singled and the new platform was built over one of the track beds. The line was redoubled and electrified as part of the Airdrie-Bathgate project, and there are now two rebuilt platforms. The original station had closed in 1956.
Uphall annual passenger numbers: 581,590

VALLEY Isle of Anglesey   15 Mar 1982
Y FALI   Sir Ynys Môn

This station is on the western tip of Anglesey nearest to Holyhead and was reopened with the benefit of a £15,000 grant from Gwynedd County Council, Ynys Môn Borough and four community councils. The original station had closed in 1966.
Valley annual passenger numbers: 16,006

WALLYFORD East Lothian   13 Jun 1994

Opened with funding from Lothian Regional Council, this new station on the East Coast main line is served by electric Edinburgh to North Berwick services. In 2008, a park-and-choose (to ride by train or bus) facility added 321 extra parking spaces, 13 spaces for disabled drivers and 10 cycle parking slots. It was part of a £5 million scheme set up by the South East of Scotland Transport Partnership.
Wallyford annual passenger numbers: 311,890

WALSDEN West Yorkshire   10 Sep 1990

Situated in the Calder Valley on the edge of the Pennines and served by Halifax-Rochdale trains, this new station reopened at a cost of £240,000 and is served by Halifax-Rochdale trains. The original station had closed in 1961.
Walsden annual passenger numbers: 102,324

WARWICK PARKWAY Warwickshire   08 Oct 2000

Owned by Chiltern Railways, this station with twin 218-metre platforms, is 2km west of Warwick at the foot of Hatton bank and has a 900-space car park readily accessible from the nearby M40 motorway. Buses serve Warwick, Leamington, Kenilworth and Coventry. The station opened at a cost of £5.5 million and by October 2002 approximately 400 passengers per day were passing through. Chiltern Railways paid for the station because Network Rail's price for building it was too high. The car park has had to be enlarged twice and Warwickshire County Council has paid for the waiting shelter to be extended to cope with demand.
Warwick Parkway annual passenger numbers: 632,234

WATERLOO INTERNATIONAL

See London Waterloo International

WATFORD STADIUM Hertfordshire   04 Dec 1982

Opened to serve football fans at Watford Football Club ground, this station was used only on match days by special trains and did not appear in the public timetable. The single platform cost £200,000 and was paid for by £54,000 from the Football Trust, Watford FC and Watford Borough Council. The station, on the disused Watford High Street to Croxley Green line, closed in 1996.

WATLINGTON Norfolk   05 May 1975

Reopened just a few years after being closed, the intact station was repainted and refurbished with lighting and fencing at a cost of £700 to villagers plus a £150 contribution from Norfolk County Council. Subsequently the London-bound platform was moved to the other side of the level crossing. The station is on the King's Lynn to Ely line and before closure in 1969 had been renamed Magdalen Road instead of its original 19th century name of Watlington. At the time, a minute was added to the timetable for diesel multiple units and three minutes for locomotive-hauled trains. The return of the railway station and electrification of the route in 1992 has resulted in many new houses being built in the village.
Watlington annual passenger numbers: 148,928

WATTON-AT-STONE Hertfordshire   17 May 1982

Costing £140,000, this rebuilt station on the Hertford loop opened after a notable campaign by local residents. During their three-year battle, villagers and well-wishers raised £4,000, the parish council provided £6,000, the district council produced £9,000 and the balance was met by British Rail and Hertfordshire County Council. The station's twin platforms can accommodate six-car electric trains and the line links Stevenage and Hertford. The original station had closed in 1939.
Watton-at-Stone annual passenger numbers: 174,696

WAUN-GRON PARK Cardiff   02 Nov 1987
PARC WAUN-GRON Caerdydd

Experimentally opened on the new Cardiff City line, the two staggered platforms costing £180,000 were funded by the former South Glamorgan County Council.
Waun-Gron Park annual passenger numbers: 78,000

WAVERTREE TECHNOLOGY PARK Liverpool   13 Aug 2000

This £2 million two-platform station is east of Edge Hill on the Earlestown line.
Wavertree Technology Park annual passenger numbers: 515,428

97

WELHAM GREEN Hertfordshire   29 Sep 1986

This Great Northern suburban station, between Brookmans Park and Hatfield, opened at a cost of £265,000, which provided twin six-car platforms on the slow lines of the East Coast main line with shelters, ticket office and car parking. It was funded jointly by Welwyn District Council, Hertfordshire County Council, Hatfield Parish Council and British Rail.
Welham Green annual passenger numbers: 212,702

WEST BROMPTON Greater London   30 May 1999

This £1.25 million reopened station on the West London line between Chelsea and Olympia has been entirely rebuilt alongside the existing London Underground District line station. It has two platforms designed for four-coach trains and is linked by a ramped footbridge and lifts to the District line station. The station was funded by the London Borough of Hammersmith and Fulham and the Royal Borough of Kensington and Chelsea. The original station closed in 1940.
West Brompton annual passenger numbers: 5,625,750

WEST HAM High Level Greater London   30 May 1999

This station opened on the London, Tilbury and Southend line to offer interchange with three London Underground services and the lower level North London line station. Situated parallel to the London Underground District line platforms, the 12-car island platform has a long waiting shelter, lifts and stairs. The new £3 million station accompanied a £75 million modernisation of the LT&S route and investment in new trains. An earlier station had closed in 1962.
West Ham annual passenger numbers (combining high and low level) : 8,778,194

WEST HAM Low Level Greater London   14 May 1979

This station is on the North London line, between Stratford and Canning Town in the London Borough of Newham. It has an island platform with basic shelters alongside the London Underground Jubilee line platforms which opened in late 1999. It closed temporarily, and reopened in 2010 as part of the Docklands Light Railway route from Canning Town to Stratford International.
West Ham annual passenger numbers (combining high and low level) : 8,778,194

WESTER HAILES Edinburgh   11 May 1987

Serving a population of 12,000 alongside the Edinburgh-Shotts-Glasgow line, this new station opened experimentally. It is adjacent to a new shopping centre and located between Kingsknowe and Kirknewton. The cost of £165,000 was met by Lothian Regional Council.
Wester Hailes annual passenger numbers: 38,644

WETHERAL Cumbria — 05 Oct 1981

For just £6,000, this station 4.5km east of Carlisle was reopened. It is served by Carlisle-Newcastle trains. The station had closed in 1967.
Wetheral annual passenger numbers: 21,474

WHALLEY Lancashire — 29 May 1994

This station reopened for a new service on the Blackburn-Clitheroe line, 32 years after the original station had closed. Whalley annual passenger numbers: 71,782

WHIFFLET North Lanarkshire — 21 Dec 1992

Opened in preparation for the reopening to passengers of the Glasgow-Rutherglen-Whifflet freight-only line, the station is on the Motherwell-Stirling line, close to the site of the original station which had closed in 1962. The station is served by half-hourly diesel trains on the Glasgow-Whifflet service, electric trains in peak hours on the Argyle line (Lanark-Larkhall-Motherwell) and hourly diesel trains on the Motherwell-Cumbernauld service.
Whifflet annual passenger numbers: 247,372

WHINHILL Inverclyde — 14 May 1990

Located in Greenock on the Wemyss Bay to Glasgow electrified line, this new single-platform station cost £258,000. Upper Greenock station closed in 1967.
Whinhill annual passenger numbers: 53,558

WHISTON Merseyside — 01 Oct 1990

This new station is located between Huyton and Rainhill on the Liverpool-Earlestown-Manchester line. The two 107-metre platforms and basic facilities cost £420,000, which was shared between Merseyside Passenger Transport Executive and Knowsley Borough Council. Whiston annual passenger numbers: 370,380

WHITWELL Derbyshire — 24 May 1998

This is the northernmost of 11 new stations along the very successful Robin Hood line which opened in three stages from Nottingham to Worksop. The original Whitwell station, which had closed in 1964, was dismantled and rebuilt at the Midland Railway Centre in Butterley.
Whitwell annual passenger numbers: 18,934

WILDMILL Bridgend — 12 Dec 1992
Y FELIN WYLLT Pen-y-bont ar Ogwr

This station opened a little later than the five other Maesteg line stations, because

last-minute modifications had to be made to the platforms to comply with health and safety legislation.
Wildmill annual passenger numbers: 22,446

WILLINGTON Derbyshire   26 May 1995

Located 8km north of Burton-on-Trent, this new station opened with two 80-metre platforms. The cost of £565,000 was funded by Derbyshire County Council and South Derbyshire District Council. The station was for many years branded as part of the Ivanhoe line project, anticipating reopening of the Leicester-Burton route. Repton and Willington station had closed in 1968.
Willington annual passenger numbers: 29,506

WINNERSH TRIANGLE Berkshire   12 May 1986

This new station on the Reading-Wokingham-Guildford line lies north of Winnersh station. The cost of £375,000 was met from contributions of £150,000 from Berkshire County Council, £150,000 from British Rail and £75,000 from Wimpey/Slough Estates. It is adjacent to an extensive new office and housing development and has a large car park.
Winnersh Triangle annual passenger numbers: 516,284

WOODSMOOR Greater Manchester   01 Oct 1990

The twin timber platforms in Stockport cost £300,000 and are served by trains on the Stockport-Buxton line.
Woodsmoor annual passenger numbers: 232,954

WORKINGTON NORTH Cumbria   30 Nov 2009

This temporary station, 1.5km north of Workington station, was built quickly after the road bridge over the River Derwent was swept away 10 days earlier. It cost Network Rail around £300,000. Allerdale Borough Council waived its right to require planning permission to avoid delaying the station opening. Train services between Workington, Workington North, Flimby and Maryport were free of charge until the end of 2009. The temporary station closed on 8 October 2010.

WORLE Weston-super-Mare   24 Sep 1990

Featuring four-car platforms and a large car park, this new £700,000 station opened to serve Weston-super-Mare to Bristol trains. In 2006 North Somerset Council undertook a £5 million upgrade of the station to allow long-distance trains to call and a larger car park.
Worle annual passenger numbers: 299,014

WREXHAM CENTRAL Wrexham   23 Nov 1998
WREXHAM CYFFREDINOL Wrecsam

A new single-platform terminus station was opened 300 metres west of the former station to enable the branch to be truncated for a retail development. This development was supported by *The Best of Both Worlds*, a Railfuture Wales 1996 publication.

Wrexham Central annual passenger numbers: 73,180

Y

YARM Stockton-on-Tees   20 Feb 1996

The twin platforms of this new station on the Northallerton-Middlesbrough line cost £670,000 and opened to TransPennine services. A 74-space car park is also provided. The original station had closed in 1960.   Yarm annual passenger numbers: 135,364

YATE South Gloucestershire   15 May 1989

The twin two-car platforms at Yate on the Bristol-Gloucester line cost £130,000 and were funded jointly by Avon County Council, Northavon District Council and British Rail. During early 1992 the county council funded a £124,000 extension of the platforms to take four-car trains. The original station had closed in 1965.

Yate annual passenger numbers: 368,910

YNYSWEN Rhondda Cynon Taf   29 Sep 1986

Between Treherbert and Treorchy, this £50,000 station was experimentally opened by the former Mid Glamorgan County Council with a single platform and shelter and is served by trains along the Rhondda Valley. The station has achieved a more than three-fold increase over forecast traffic.

Ynyswen annual passenger numbers: 9,376

YSTRAD RHONDDA Rhondda Cynon Taf   29 Sep 1986

An earlier station named Ystrad Rhondda was renamed Ton Pentre and is the next station up the Rhondda Valley. The new Ystrad Rhondda station has two 91-metre platforms with a passing loop on this single-track line. The station is served by Treherbert-Cardiff trains, and since opening its usage has increased four-fold to over 500 passengers per day.

Ystrad Rhondda annual passenger numbers: 44,600

Explanatory notes

Dates: Official opening dates and the date when the station was first used by regular passenger trains sometimes differ. We have normally used the date when the station opened for passengers.

New and reopened: Many of the stations listed are reopenings, although sometimes not on exactly the same site as the original station. Some of the stations listed are entirely new or are significantly enlarged, such as Ashford International.

Distances: Distances have been rendered in kilometres and may have been rounded. The railway is moving towards metric measurements, which are already used on High Speed 1 and Heathrow Express, and will probably be used on new lines in future.

Platform lengths: Platforms are sometimes described as suitable for two-car or four-car trains but coach lengths do vary. For instance, a two-car class 158 unit which has 23-metre coaches cannot always use a two-car platform designed for a class 150 unit which has shorter 20-metre coaches.

Local authorities: Local government areas and names have changed over the years and so common usage has been retained in some cases. However many former counties have been retained, including West Midlands, because this is the name of the passenger transport authority.

Names: Even station names are sometimes inconsistent. For Wales, we have usually taken the station name that appears on the station signs, but these can be at variance with those in the Arriva Trains Wales pocket timetables and the Network Rail database.

Experimental: Some stations are noted as experimental openings. This refers to the Speller amendment to the 1962 Transport Act which allows rail companies to reopen stations without having to comply with the statutory closure procedures if the experiment does not live up to expectations.

Developer funding: Reference is also made to section 106 agreements, which allow local authorities to make agreements under the 1990 Town and Country Planning Act with developers to provide funding for rail stations.

Annual passenger numbers: The annual passenger numbers quoted for each reopened station are for 2015-16. They are taken from the Office of Rail and Road estimates. Railfuture campaigners have been critical of these figures in the past, particularly those for London stations, because ORR appeared not to take full account of passengers who were travelling legally but without traditional paper tickets. ORR has listened to the criticism and the current ORR data seem to be more accurate.

Railfuture has made every effort to ensure that material is accurate and up-to-date but cannot be held responsible for any errors or omissions.

Stations opening soon

CANARY WHARF London   Expected 2018

Picture: Crossrail

CANARY WHARF: The Crossrail station at Canary Wharf nearing completion in 2015, six years after construction started. The glazed roof contains a garden which sits atop five floors. Beneath the five-storey development are the Crossrail platforms

Crossrail's Canary Wharf station is the third station to serve the London Docklands financial district. The Crossrail station is at the bottom of a five-storey development known as Crossrail Place which was built by the Canary Wharf Group. The 250 metre-long station box is 18 metres below the water level of West India Quay dock, as shown in the artist's impression of the development (pictured right).
Canary Wharf already has one station on the Docklands Light Railway and another on the Underground's Jubilee line.
The Crossrail station has an unusual timber lattice roof over a roof garden which is partly open to the sky and partly covered.
The station is expected to open in December

Picture: Crossrail

2018 and when Crossrail (now known as the Elizabeth line) is fully operational in December 2019, there will be a train every five minutes at peak time to Paddington, Heathrow or Reading in the west and Abbey Wood in the east.
See Chapter 5: Lines opening soon, London Crossrail

BARKING RIVERSIDE   Expected 2019

A station at Barking Riverside is expected when the line from Gospel Oak to Barking is extended to serve an area where more than 10,000 homes are planned. Construction of the station could start in 2017 for opening by the end of 2019.
See Chapter 5: Lines opening soon, Barking Riverside Link

BEAM PARK London   Expected 2020

Beam Park station will be built on the site of Ford's derelict factory, between Dagenham Dock and Rainham, downriver from Barking. The station will be on the c2c route, 20 minutes from London's Fenchurch Street station. The 29-hectare site, bisected by the Beam River, will accommodate at least 2,000 new homes and possibly up to 5,000 in associated nearby developments. The station is to be built in partnership with Network Rail, the franchise operator c2c, and £9 million from Transport for London. The station was part of the negotiations for the new Essex Thameside rail franchise in 2014.

BEAULIEU PARK Chelmsford, Essex   Expected 2022

Beaulieu in Chelmsford could open on the Great Eastern main line in 2021 or 2022 as part of the 850-acre Beaulieu Park providing 3,500 new homes near the A12/A130 road interchange. Network Rail signed a memorandum of understanding with developers in December 2015 to deliver the station on a 50:50 basis. The station is designed to also have a park-and-ride function.

BROADWAY Worcestershire   Expected 2018

The popular Cotswold village of Broadway will be accessible by rail when this station on the preserved steam and diesel Gloucestershire Warwickshire Railway opens in 2018. Broadway lost its station in 1960.
See Chapter 5: Lines opening soon, Laverton-Broadway

DALCROSS Inverness   Expected 2019

A new £5.6 million station at Dalcross will serve Inverness Airport. In July 2015, the plan was for a 150-space car park and platforms on the Inverness-Aberdeen line but talks were under way to see how the station and airport could be integrated for seamless connections. The Aberdeen-Inverness line is undergoing a £170 million upgrade over the next four years, involving 16 kilometres of double tracking and signalling improvements. Originally the upgrade was planned for implementation in 2007.

EAST LINTON East Lothian   Expected 2018

In 2016, the South East of Scotland Transport Partnership, Scottish Borders and East Lothian councils increased their proposed funding to unprecedented levels towards the £11 million cost of reopening East Linton station and establishing a local rail service between Edinburgh and Berwick-upon-Tweed which Rail Action Group East of Scotland say would be a "huge benefit to the local economy". Network Rail has carried out preliminary design work on a station at East Linton to replace the one that closed in 1964 and another proposed station at Reston. Abellio ScotRail, which took over the franchise in April 2015, has committed to reopening East Linton and Reston stations. Rail campaigner Barrie Forrest, 74, who was awarded the British Empire Medal in January 2017, was involved with the reopening campaign, which included a petition to the Scottish Parliament in 2014.
See also Reston in this chapter

EDGINSWELL Devon   Expected 2018

A new station at Edginswell, Torquay, is part of the county council's Devon Metro plan to create an alternative to car use. The station would serve Torbay Hospital, the Willows retail park and Torquay Gateway development area. The £9 million station will be built between Newton Abbot and Torre. The station could open in 2018 and is being funded by Torbay Council and the Department for Transport through the Heart of the South West Local Enterprise Partnership. On completion of new stations at Edginswell and Marsh Barton, reopened stations at Cullompton and Wellington may follow. They are supported by the Local Authorities in Devon and Somerset at both District and County level.

GREEN PARK Reading   Expected December 2018

Work is expected to start in 2017 on the £8 million station at Reading Green Park which should open in 2018. Delays to the electrification of the Reading-Basingstoke line created uncertainty around the project. Phase 1 will provide a station with two five-coach platforms, platform canopies and a footbridge. Three other phases will

GREEN PARK: Artist's impression of the Reading station

105

expand the facilities later. The Department for Transport gave the go-ahead for this station in 2006, but scaled-back development plans put the station on hold for several years. The scheme is funded by the local enterprise partnership and local authority contributions including Section 106 payments.

HAXBY York   Expected ?

Funding for reopening Haxby station was announced in 2009, with a target date for opening in January 2013, but the plans were put on hold in 2010 because of funding worries. The station has a catchment area of 23,000 people The possibility of reopening Haxby was revived by York Council in 2012. The new station is expected to be built near the site of the original station, which lost its regular passenger service in 1930. In March 2015, MP Julian Sturdy said the reopening had moved a step closer, following a meeting with Claire Perry, the rail minister at the time.

KENILWORTH Warwickshire   Expected December 2017

Work to rebuild this Leamington-Coventry line station began in September 2009 but was halted when funding was refused. Work re-started again in 2015 and the station should open in 2017 after signalling improvements by Network Rail. The £12 million reopening project is being funded by the Department for Transport, Coventry & Warwickshire local enterprise partnership and Warwickshire County Council. The population of Kenilworth has more than tripled since the 1965 closure. Two preserved stained glass windows from the original station ticket office have been incorporated into the design of the new building. Local primary school children have also created more than 300 posters to decorate the outside of the new station.

Picture: Warwickshire County Council

KENILWORTH: An artist's impression of how the station will look

KINTORE: A 1973 picture of the station, which closed in 1964. Since then Kintore's population has expanded and there are also plans for the line to be redoubled

KINTORE Aberdeenshire   Expected 2019

Aberdeenshire Council officials are working with Network Rail and the North East of Scotland Transport Partnership to develop a new station at Kintore to replace one that closed in 1964. Successive Scottish transport ministers have indicated their support for a Kintore station and now, more than 30 years after Dyce station reopened, it is hoped the station will open in time for the completion of a £170 million redoubling of the Aberdeen-Inverness line. Campaigners say the Aberdeen commuter service should be extended to Kintore.

MAGHULL NORTH Merseyside   Expected 2018

Merseyrail is planning to open a second rail station at Maghull. The new £7.3 million station will be located just off School lane, between the existing Maghull and Town Green stations on the Liverpool-Ormskirk line. It will help meet demand from an adjacent new housing development of 370 homes. The station will have a 156-space car park. Work is set to start on site in August 2017 to cope with growing demand on the Merseyrail network. The Government offered £6 million via the Local Growth Fund, with £700,000 from Merseytravel and £500,000 from the Housing and Communities Agency, which is developing land on the east side of the railway.

MARSH BARTON Devon   Expected 2018

A new £7 million Marsh Barton railway station between Exeter St Thomas and Starcross was approved in July 2015 and will form part of the county council's Devon Metro plans. The proposed site for two platforms has been cleared. It falls in a strategic employment area and is expected to support employment development.

PILL Somerset   Expected 2020

Pill station will be reopened when the Bristol-Portishead line is back in action for passenger use in 2020. Land for the station was agreed in 2016. Local councils are hoping the new station will result in reduced car usage in Pill and surrounding villages.
See also Chapter 5: Lines opening soon

RESTON East Lothian   Expected 2018

Abellio took over the ScotRail franchise in April 2015 and committed to reopening Reston and East Linton stations as well as running an Edinburgh to Berwick-upon-Tweed local service. However it claims it cannot run the service until 2018 because of a shortage of diesel trains. The reopening campaign has been led by Rail Action Group East of Scotland.
See also East Linton

Picture: Barrie Forrest

RESTON: The site on the Edinburgh-Berwick section of the East Coast main line

ROBROYSTON   Expected 2019

Glasgow is set to open its 60th railway station at Robroyston on the Queen Street line to Cumbernauld. The £19 million park-and-ride station will provide a rail service for both Robroyston and the Millerston area where 1,600 new homes are to be built. It is the first to be funded through the £30 million Scottish Stations Fund, which was announced in 2014. Glasgow City Council is providing £10 million, Transport Scotland will contribute £7 million, Strathclyde Passenger Transport £1.25 million, while developers will contribute the remaining £485,000.

SOHAM   Expected 2024

Soham station could reopen at a cost of more than £6 million after funding was offered by the Greater Cambridge Greater Peterborough Local Enterprise Partnership, according to press reports in January 2017. But the LEP's offer of £2.2 million was dependent on the Department for Transport agreeing to earmark £2.5 million from its New Stations Fund, and £2 million from the new combined authority for Cambridge and Peterborough.

It is also dependent on Network Rail doubling the existing single line between Soham and Ely and other improvements at Ely North, which could cost £200 million and are expected to be carried out between 2019 and 2024. NR has proposed funding Soham, Soham-Ely doubling, Ely area works, and Wisbech reinstatement as one package. The train operator Greater Anglia has plans to introduce an hourly Ipswich-Peterborough service over the line through Soham. Soham station opened in 1879, but closed to passenger traffic in 1965. It was badly damaged in 1944, after a trainload of bombs caught fire and exploded.

RUGBY PARKWAY Warwickshire   Expected 2019

A new £11 million Rugby Parkway station at Hillmorton was approved in October 2015 by Warwickshire County Council. It will be built on the A428 Crick Road, on the old radio mast site, near Daventry International Rail Freight Terminal, and will serve a new housing development of up to 6,200 homes between existing housing and the Daventry International Rail Freight Terminal. The station will connect to the Northampton loop of the West Coast main line with trains to Birmingham, Northampton, the West Midlands and London, and it will have a 260-space car park. The council will contribute £2 million to the project, and bid for £4.9 million from the Government's new stations fund, with £3.9 million from the Coventry & Warwickshire Local Enterprise Partnership Growth Deal. Work is expected to begin in 2018.

WARRINGTON WEST Cheshire   Expected 2018

Warrington Borough Council wants to build a £12.5 million two-platform park-and-ride station to serve the new Chapelford urban village between Warrington Central and Sankey for Penketh stations. In mid 2016, the council was seeking additional funding because of cost increases. Four trains an hour are expected to serve the new station, which will support six-car trains to both Liverpool and Manchester, with passive provision for eight-car trains in the future. It will have space for 300 cars and 100 cycles.

WIXAMS Bedfordshire   Expected 2020

Before the housing slump, December 2010 was the target date for opening this four-platform station at Elstow/Wixams, located 5km south of Bedford on the Midland main line on a site provided by developer Gallaghers, which said it was prepared to contribute £13.5 million. In June 2017, the cost of a station at Wixams was estimated at £30 million. Based on the site of the former Elstow Storage Depot, Wixams will be home to 10,000 people. Residents staged a protest in March 2015, saying they had been promised a new station. The station, on the borders of Bedford Borough and Central Bedfordshire, has been designed and the developers were said to be "working closely" with Network Rail. The Highways Agency upgraded and dualled the A6 trunk road past The Wixams even before houses were built but the railway authorities have failed to deliver the station. Planning consent for the rail station was obtained in 2012. Because of "the lack of available funding", this lapsed in 2015. A fresh application will be needed once the form of the station is agreed, funding secured and the precise route of East West Rail is fixed.

WORCESTER PARKWAY Worcestershire   Expected 2019

Planning permission for the £22 million Worcester Parkway station near Norton and junction 7 of the M5 was approved in 2015. The county council said construction of the station would be a flagship regeneration project. It will have a single platform on the Cotswold line and two on the Birmingham-Bristol Line and is being funded by the county council and £8.3 million from the Worcestershire local enterprise partnership. It is expected to have 500 car park spaces. Most of the cost of the scheme is expected to be recouped through station car park fees and access charges levied on train operating companies. The Cotswold Line Promotion Group has expressed its concerns about the viability of a new Worcester Parkway station, which could threaten the viability of other local stations.

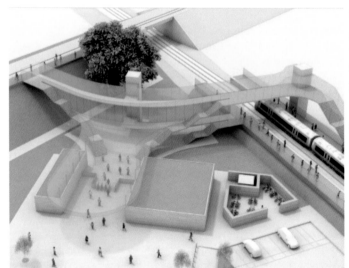

WORCESTER PARKWAY: An artist's impression of the station

Chapter 4

New lines for passengers

In addition to the many stations opened along existing passenger routes, an increasing number of services have been introduced on former freight-only lines or via newly constructed tracks. Some case studies are outlined here.

BATHGATE-NEWBRIDGE JUNCTION (Edinburgh)   1986

The 16km of residual freight line from Newbridge Junction on the main Edinburgh-Glasgow line reopened for passenger trains to Bathgate in 1986 (after a break of 30 years) thanks to the inspired leadership of Chris Green, then ScotRail's general manager and now Railfuture vice-president. Although the creation of a fast surface link from Edinburgh to the planned Livingston New Town had been discussed for decades, Chris Green made it happen with the reopened Bathgate line and creation of a Livingston North station. Uphall station opened at the same time. By 2010, the line was carrying four times as many passengers as the experts had predicted. Without the 1986 reopening, we would probably never have seen Bathgate-Airdrie reopening in 2010.

WALSALL-RUGELEY TRENT VALLEY   1989-1998

The 25km line between Walsall and Rugeley Trent Valley closed to passengers in 1965 but remained open to freight. It reopened for passengers in stages from 1989 to 1998. Walsall-Hednesford reopened in 1989, Hednesford-Rugeley Town in 1997 and Rugeley Town-Rugeley Trent Valley in 1998. In 2017, the line was being electrified at a cost of £78 million, which will allow journey times to be cut and diesel trains freed up for transfer elsewhere. The line speed will also be increased from 72kph to 120kph.

ROBIN HOOD LINE   08 May 1993 - 20 Nov 1995 - 24 May 1998

Claimed as the most successful reopened line in England, attracting more than one million passengers a year, this line reopened in three phases. First the 17km route from Nottingham to Newstead, which was extended by 8km to Mansfield Woodhouse as Phase 2, with a final 21km extension to Worksop comprising Phase 3. A reinstated stretch of railway was built between Kirkby-in-Ashfield and Newstead and a filled-in tunnel had to be excavated. Until the reopening, Mansfield was one of the largest towns in Britain without a rail station. Sunday services were introduced from December 2008, with funding by Nottinghamshire County Council.

WALSALL-WOLVERHAMPTON   24 May 1998

A passenger service was reintroduced on this 10km freight line. Previously passengers from Wolverhampton had to take a train to Birmingham New Street and change on to another to Walsall. The one-hour journey time was slashed to just 13 minutes with the direct link, with no intermediate stations. However, due to poor publicity and an irregular hourly service, usage was lower than expected. The service was withdrawn in 2008, apart from a token parliamentary train. In 2017 Railfuture is still campaigning for reintroduction of direct Walsall-Wolverhampton services. Walsall Council is committed to reintroduce the service and plans to investigate the possibility of new stations at Willenhall, Portobello and Darlaston. Railfuture believes extending the present Walsall-Birmingham-Wolverhampton back to Walsall direct could be the best way forward.

HEATHROW EXPRESS   23 Jun 1998

Heathrow Express is a 160kph premium-price rail link offering a journey time from Paddington to Heathrow Airport Terminals 1/2/3 of just 15 minutes, and Terminal 5 in a further six minutes. Terminal 4 is served directly by a 37-minute Heathrow Connect service stopping at main line stations, but can be reached in 23 minutes by changing at Terminals 1/2/3. However, a proposed St Pancras-Heathrow Express service via Cricklewood has never materialised.

Electric trains run over 19km of the main line from Paddington to Airport junction, near Hayes, and then for 8km beneath the airport in tunnels that cost £60 million. The original £350 million project, a joint venture between BAA and the British Railways Board, was designed to increase use of public transport to and from the airport from 34% to 50%. From 19 January to 25 May 1998, following a tunnel collapse during construction, a temporary service ran between Paddington and a single-platform station, Heathrow Junction, just north of the tunnel into the airport. Each railway carriage was labelled for a specific terminal, and at Heathrow Junction passengers transferred to four similarly labelled buses.

Prime Minister Tony Blair officially opened the full Heathrow Express service on 23 June 1998. The train sets soon had to be strengthened to operate in nine-car formations, a five-car and a four-car train coupled together. On 27 March 2008, the terminus changed from Terminal 4 to the new Terminal 5, which was reached via twin 1.7km tunnels built at the same time as those for London Underground. Platforms 3 and 4 of Terminals 1/2/3 serve Heathrow Express, and 5 and 6 the Piccadilly Tube line. Initially screened by a wall, platforms 1 and 2 provide for a future Airtrack spur from the Staines-Waterloo line, that could form part of a through route. The total cost of the project, including design, supply and installation of railway, was £118 million. BAA owns the stations and the line, but they are managed by Network Rail, which controls the entire route. Crossrail will link Heathrow to Shenfield and Docklands via the same route, and will have an interchange with HS2 at Old Oak Common, but Heathrow will still be at a disadvantage as the only major European hub airport not served directly by a high-speed railway.

See also Chapter 5: Lines opening soon, Heathrow western link

HALIFAX-HUDDERSFIELD/SOWERBY BRIDGE-MIRFIELD
28 May 2000

Financed by West Yorkshire Passenger Transport Authority, this 11km of track enabled the reinstatement of a local passenger service between Halifax and Huddersfield, withdrawn in 1970. Only one closed intermediate station, Brighouse, was reopened, while a second at Elland, which closed in 1962, was abandoned because of low estimates of use. However a property developer has since offered to fund its reopening which could cost up to £3 million, and is supported by the Halifax and District Rail Action Group. Although an indirect route, the line itself offers connectional opportunities to Bradford and Sheffield. An hourly service between Manchester Victoria and Leeds via Brighouse and Mirfield was introduced over this line in December 2008.

PORTOBELLO JUNCTION-NEWCRAIGHALL   03 Jun 2002

This 2.5km line was reopened to passengers as Edinburgh Crossrail, with direct trains connecting Newcraighall in the east with the Edinburgh-Glenrothes-Edinburgh Fife Circle service. This is now part of the Borders Railway route, which allows trains to travel beyond Newcraighall to Tweedbank.
See also Edinburgh-Tweedbank in this chapter

SWANSEA DISTRICT LINE Cwrt Sart Jct-Morlais Jct   Jun 2002

This previously freight-only line has been used since 2002 by services from Newport to West Wales, allowing trains to bypass Neath, Skewen, Llansamlet, Swansea and Gowerton. There have also been Cardiff to Builth Wells services for the annual Royal Welsh Show and charter trains to West Wales and the Heart of Wales line. RailfutureCymru/Wales argues for a direct service by this route from Carmarthen to London Paddington, with new rail/road interchange stations at Llandarcy, Morriston and Pontarddulais. The line runs from Cwrt Sart junction at Briton Ferry on the South Wales main line to Morlais junction near Pontarddulais

HIGH-SPEED 1
Channel Tunnel Rail Link

Phase 1 74km **28 Sep 2003**
Phase 2 39km **14 Nov 2007**

French Railways (SNCF) had its high-speed rail link ready in 1993, a year before the Channel Tunnel opened, while the Belgian high-speed branch was completed in 1997. It took Britain until September 2003 to open its first stretch of high-speed railway, from the tunnel to Fawkham junction, and another four years to complete the tunnelling into the completely refurbished St Pancras International station.
The full 109km route, plus the short link to the existing network used between 2003 and 2007, and including the new depot at Temple Mills, cost £5,800 million. Bi-directional throughout, it

HIGH SPEED ONE: This 2003 picture shows a 1km viaduct under construction at Thurrock, Essex, to take the Channel Tunnel rail link, now known as HS1, over a dual carriageway road. This part of the rail link to St Pancras opened four years later

has 152 bridges and viaducts and 24km of tunnelling. Domestic 140kph Javelin trains started running from eastern Kent stations from December 2009 and have been a great success.

Conservative Prime Minister John Major expected the private sector to pay for the line, but on this occasion the private sector proved risk averse. John Prescott as deputy prime minister in the Labour government of Tony Blair arranged the government financial guarantee that allowed the project to be successfully undertaken.

HS1 TERMINUS: St Pancras International with a Eurostar emerging from the new flat-roof extension catering for inter-city and domestic high-speed services

DORE SOUTH CURVE   May 2003-Sep 2004

From May 2003 to September 2004, while services on the West Coast main line were disrupted by major engineering work, a London St Pancras-Manchester service operated via a reopened Dore South curve and the scenic Edale valley. The IC125 service went via the Midland main line as far as Trent junction, before taking the Erewash Valley Line (avoiding Derby) to Clay Cross, rejoining the Midland main line until Dore South curve.

EASTLEIGH-ROMSEY   18 May 2003

The single-track freight line between Romsey and Eastleigh in Hampshire was reopened to passengers in 2003, along with the new station at Chandler's Ford which had lost its passenger service in 1969. The reopened station now has a quarter of a million passengers a year.

115

Picture: Bettina Skovbro

BREAKTHROUGH: A train breaks through the barrier at Bridgend station to mark the reopening of the Vale of Glamorgan line, which was a £17 million project. The line opened to regular passenger services two days after the official opening

BARRY *Y Barri* to BRIDGEND *Pen-y-bont ar Ogwr*   12 Jun 2005

In 1977, a Railfuture Wales booklet *Rails to the Vale* advocated reopening this 30.5km Vale of Glamorgan freight line, which closed to passenger use in 1964 except for the occasional diversion. Network Rail and the Welsh Government spent £12 million on two new stations at Llantwit Major and Rhoose, a reinstated bay platform at Bridgend, and upgraded infrastructure including extra signals. In 2005 the line reopened, and attracted 225,000 passenger journeys in its first 12 months. Railfuture celebrated with a conference in Barry.

MARYHILL-ANNIESLAND   29 Sep 2005

This short stretch of new line allowed an improved service on the North Glasgow suburban line and included a new station at Kelvindale. The freight-only line had closed in 1988 after local trains ended in 1917 and remaining passenger services were withdrawn in 1951. It reopened in 2005 as a 1.5km single line extension of the

116

suburban line with an intermediate station at Kelvindale. Trains from Glasgow Queen Street terminated in a new bay platform at Anniesland. This line is still operated by diesel trains. The Maryhill line was to have been been electrified as part of the Edinburgh Glasgow Improvement Programme but was dropped.

HAUGHEAD JCT (Hamilton Central) to LARKHALL 12 Dec 2005

Closed to passengers in 1965, and freight in 1968, this 4.7km section of the former line to Strathaven was rebuilt with stations at Chatelherault, Merryton and Larkhall (formerly Central). It is an electrified single track with a passing loop at Lanark road bridge and double track at Larkhall. The Larkhall-Milngavie service immediately exceeded targets, and by 2008 trains were carrying around 40% more passengers than predicted, prompting Strathclyde Partnership for Transport to sanction £50,000 for a study into extending the line to Stonehouse.

EBBW VALLEY LINE *Lein Glyn Ebwy*   06 Feb 2008

The Ebbw Valley line closed to passengers in 1962 and was little used after October 2002. The original £30 million project involved upgrading the existing Western Valley line and also 29km of the Ebbw Vale-Newport freight-only branch. Track works began in September 2006, and the passenger service from Ebbw Vale to Cardiff avoiding Newport resumed in 2008. Stations opened at Ebbw Vale Parkway, Newbridge, Rogerstone and Risca & Pontymister initially, followed by Llanhilleth and Crosskeys. Jointly funded by the Welsh Government, an objective 1 grant from the European Union and the coalfield regeneration fund, the project was promoted by Blaenau Gwent Council, as lead authority, and Caerphilly Council, which was the first time a local authority had responsibility for commissioning and building a railway line.

By October 2009, the line had carried its millionth passenger, against the 400,000 expected. It was extended by 2.5km to a new station at Ebbw Vale Town in 2015, when work began on a £40 million enhancement scheme to improve Llanhilleth and Newbridge stations and dual the track between Crosskeys and Aberbeeg junctions. A second phase proposed by Blaenau Gwent would upgrade a chord for passenger trains to restore a service from Ebbw Vale to Newport. The project would involve some line redoubling and a second platform at both Llanhilleth and Newbridge, and could be completed by 2018.

STIRLING-ALLOA-KINCARDINE   19 May 2008

Passenger services ended on this line in 1968, but the section between Stirling and Cambus was used for freight until 1993. The 11km from Stirling to a new station at Alloa was rebuilt as 100kph single-track with two passing loops. In its first year of operation,

NOT BEYOND RESCUE: This is what the trackbed at Cambus looked like when engineers began work on reopening on the Alloa-Stirling-Kincardine line in 2005

it saw over 400,000 passengers against a target figure of 155,000. The remaining 10km between Alloa and Kincardine was also reinstated with a 45kph line speed, so that coal trains serving Longannet power station could avoid the congested Forth Bridge, which also has a weight restriction that limits the type of wagons that can be used. However, Longannet closed in March 2016. Many of the 16 under-bridges were replaced. Sensibly the route was built to W9 container gauge. Funded by Transport Scotland, the two schemes finally cost a total of £85 million, against the £35 million predicted in 2005. Much of the increase was caused by the need to stabilise mines east of Alloa, although £12 million was spent on the 1.5km Alloa East Link Road (£4 million for construction and £8 million for land acquisition) to allow a level crossing to be closed. Costs also escalated when the local authority reclassified the land around the station from "general commercial" to "prime retail".

Then, reopening was delayed when on safety grounds, the level crossing at Cambus, one of six reinstated, was belatedly changed from automatic half barrier to full barrier. A new station at Cambus has also been considered, but it is claimed that the extra minutes would have made the timetable unworkable.

The first freight train, for driver training, operated along the entire line in April 2008. On 15 May 2008, three charter trains ran to celebrate the passenger reopening. A once-a-day service from Alloa to Edinburgh via Stirling started in May 2009.
The South East Scotland Transport Partnership is investigating the feasibility of running passenger trains to Edinburgh, heading east from Alloa, either by reversing at Dunfermline Town or bypassing it via a new chord to go straight on to Edinburgh. There are also prospects for running other freight trains on the line, including sand traffic, which would need 7km of line to be relaid on the old route to Dunfermline.

OLIVE MOUNT CHORD, LIVERPOOL   06 Mar 2009

This 400-metre chord connecting the route between Liverpool Docks and the West Coast main line officially reopened in March 2009, after being closed in the 1980s. Merseytravel provided £5.6 million towards the £7.6 million link, which passes through a tunnel. It allows freight trains to and from Liverpool Docks to avoid a reversal at Edge Hill and so reduces delays to passenger trains.

CORBY-MANTON JUNCTION   27 Apr 2009
SYSTON EAST-SYSTON NORTH JUNCTIONS

Picture: Jim Wade

Two months after the reopening of Corby station in February 2009, East Midlands Trains introduced a limited daily service to Derby via Oakham which meant that regular London-Derby passenger trains returned to the 16km stretch of line from Corby to Manton junction. Until then it had been used by freight trains and diverted passenger services (often on Sundays). It meant that timetabled passenger trains

CORBY: A train with the destination 'Melton Mowbray'

also started using the 300-metre chord from Syston East to Syston North junctions, north of Leicester. Railfuture East Midlands believes that more passenger trains could be run from Kettering via Corby, Oakham and Melton Mowbray to Leicester and back down the Midland main line, with the potential for stations at Gretton, East Goscote, Thurmaston, Kibworth and Desborough. The route from Corby to Manton junction includes 82-arch Harringworth viaduct, the longest masonry structure on the UK rail network, which spans the Welland Valley on the borders of Northamptonshire and Rutland. It has undergone major refurbishment.

A new Transport for London Overground link from Clapham Junction to Highbury & Islington completed a London orbital railway and achieved the OrbiRail concept advocated by Railfuture and other groups for at least three decades. The project cost £1 billion, but was predicted to yield £10 billion in economic regeneration benefits. It incorporates disused parts of the rail network and National Rail and Underground infrastructure. At its core is the former Underground East London line, which closed in 2006 and was reconstructed and extended. The terminus at Shoreditch closed in 2006, with the line diverted north of Whitechapel via a new alignment over the main line from Liverpool Street and then over Shoreditch High Street to join the former Broad Street to Richmond and Watford line, which closed in 1986. Between Whitechapel and Dalston Junction, new stations were built at Shoreditch High Street, Hoxton, Haggerston and Dalston Junction, all with step-free access. Started in June 2005, the work involved replacing or refurbishing 22 bridges along the Shoreditch-Dalston viaduct, and a new bridge at Brick Lane over the main line from Liverpool Street.

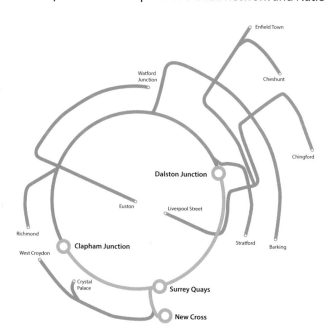

EAST LONDON LINE: Railfuture campaigned for the OrbiRail concept for more than 30 years

In September 2006, the then Mayor of London Ken Livingstone announced a further £50 million extension from Dalston Junction to Highbury & Islington, using two of the four tracks between Dalston and Highbury, in parallel with the North London line service, and connecting at Highbury & Islington with the Victoria line, and also the National Rail Moorgate to Welwyn Garden City and Hertford North services. This extension started from May 2011.

Across the Thames, at New Cross Gate, a new northbound flyover links to Network Rail's tracks, and extends the route to West Croydon and Crystal Palace, substantially enhancing the Southern service. Services from Dalston to Crystal Palace, West Croydon, New Cross and New Cross Gate started in May 2010. Phase 2 of the scheme involved a new branch south-westwards from Surrey Quays, via an abandoned freight-only route, to join the London Bridge-Peckham Rye line north of Queens Road, Peckham. Funding was approved in early 2009. London Overground trains now run via the South London line and existing freight-only curves (Factory junction-Ludgate junction) to terminate at Clapham Junction, in platforms shared with the West London line services also operated by London Overground. London's night Tube services will be extended to the East London Line in December 2017. Night trains will operate between New Cross Gate and Dalston Junction on Friday and Saturday and will be extended to Highbury & Islington in 2019.

AIRDRIE-BATHGATE   12 Dec 2010

Reopening Airdrie-Bathgate after a gap of over 50 years re-established a fourth direct rail route between Edinburgh and Glasgow, the second to be electrified. Passengers can now travel direct from Helensburgh and Milngavie in the west, and to Bathgate and Edinburgh in the east. Ron McAulay, Network Rail Director Scotland, said: "Completing this line in just four years was a major engineering and project management challenge." At this time, it was the longest new domestic passenger railway with stations that had been reopened in Britain for over a century. Transport Scotland funded the £370 million project which was estimated to bring £716 million of benefit to the local economy. It involved relaying 22km of double track between Drumgelloch, near Airdrie, North Lanarkshire, and Bathgate, West Lothian, and also redoubling and electrifying existing lines at either end of the route. The project involved 46 bridges and 13 new crossings, including six new footbridges at the stations, other foot and cycle bridges to maintain existing rights of way, and a number of new road links. The Glasgow-Drumgelloch section was already electrified as part of the Glasgow suburban network and double-tracked as far as Airdrie. However, to the east, doubling of the line from Bathgate to Newbridge junction and electrification into Edinburgh were needed. Modification works to bridges on this section accounted for some of the structures that had to be built. The 29km of operational railway needed extensive work in addition to the 24km of new link. To cater for the existing users of the route, an alternative

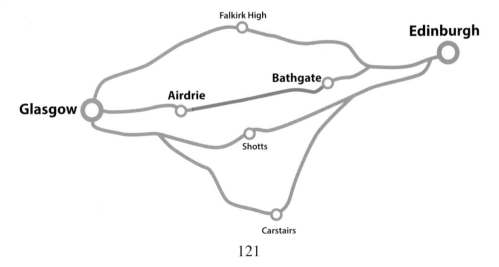

National Cycle route 75 was reinstated at a cost of £7 million. The rail route opened on 12 December 2010, but two of the three new intermediate stations (Armadale and Caldercruix, along with the relocated Drumgelloch station) had a bus replacement service until February or March 2011 because of extreme weather conditions. Blackridge (formerly Westcraigs) in West Lothian did open on schedule after the South East Scotland Regional Transport Partnership, made up of councils including Edinburgh and Fife, had secured funding in 2008 when developers Manorlane agreed to pay 40% of the £5 million cost as part of a local housing scheme.

There is also passive provision for a future additional station at Plains, between Drumgelloch and Caldercruix. The campaign for Plains goes on. Campaigner Jackie McGuire told a Railfuture

LAYING THE FINAL TRACKS: Senior project manager Hugh Wark, left, and scheme sponsor Alan Macmillan install the final 'golden' pandral clip on the Airdrie-Bathgate line in August 2010

conference in 2012 that the business case for Stirling-Alloa had been based on 85,000 users, but this figure was revised to 155,000 following the experience of the 2005 Larkhall-Hamilton (for Milngavie) reopening. After the line had reopened, a new estimate based on the initial patronage was 400,000, but by the end of 2011 even that figure had been exceeded.

NUNEATON NORTH CHORD   Nov 2012

The £28 million 1.5 km Nuneaton chord leaves the Leicester-Birmingham line at the point where it crosses the West Coast main line near Two Bridges. The chord then

Picture: Network Rail

NUNEATON NORTH CHORD: GB Railfreight managing director John Smith, left, with the then transport minister Simon Burns, Network Rail's director of freight Tim Robinson and GB Railfreight train driver Mark Winkworth at the official opening of Nuneaton North Chord in 2012. The train Is en route from Felixstowe to Barton Dock

rejoins the West Coast main line to the north of Canal Farm. Separating freight and passenger services north of Nuneaton allows freight trains to pass through the area without delaying passenger services. The chord allows high cube 9ft 6in containers to be transported from Britain's busiest port at Felixstowe to the Midlands, North West England and central Scotland.

HITCHIN flyover   26 Jun 2013

Built between 2012 and 2013 as a 2km single-track embankment and viaduct, the flyover north of Hitchin station in Hertfordshire takes northbound trains to Letchworth and Cambridge over the East Coast main line rather than across the four-track flat junction, thereby removing conflict and allowing more trains on both the main line and the line to Cambridge. A similar 1970s scheme was shelved because of budget cuts.
See also Chapter 5: Lines opening soon, Thameslink

IPSWICH Bacon Factory Chord   24 Mar 2014

This 1.2km Bacon Factory chord at Ipswich that opened in 2014 is crucial in speeding freight trains from Felixstowe to the Midlands by eliminating a bottleneck on the Great Eastern main line. Its £59 million cost was partly met by the European Union as the route forms part of the Trans-European Transport Network.
The chord was promoted by Ipswich Borough Council with Councillor Phil Smart (a Railfuture member) playing a crucial role, drawing up the scheme and winning support

HITCHIN FLYOVER: Trains from London to Cambridge and King's Lynn can now leave the East Coast main line without disrupting long-distance trains

IPSWICH BACON FACTORY CHORD: A crucial step in allowing freight trains from Felixstowe Docks to gain access to the North and Midlands by eliminating a bottleneck on the Great Eastern main line

from Felixstowe Port, the Rail Freight Group and the then Strategic Rail Authority. Eventually Network Rail was convinced. As Richard Schofield of Network Rail put it: "This project is a key part of our plans to take more freight off roads and on to rail. This project will help to take up to 750,000 lorry journeys off the road every year by 2030, reducing traffic congestion and carbon emissions as well as improving road safety."

The curve is currently used only by freight trains, but improves the efficiency of the Felixstowe line where the volume of freight trains was causing delays to the passenger service. Cllr Smart wants to see the line from Felixstowe to Birmingham electrified and the 20km Felixstowe-Ipswich East Suffolk line dualled, to allow more freight and passenger trains.

DONCASTER NORTH CHORD   03 Jun 2014

The new 3.2km chord at Shaftholme, north of Doncaster, keeps freight trains serving Immingham docks and the power stations of Drax, Ferrybridge and Eggborough clear of the East Coast main line, on which they used to run for up to 22 km. The £45 million project included a 246 metre-long viaduct, a new overbridge and underbridge, and railway embankments. It also enabled the closure of Joan Croft level crossing. Although used only by freight trains, the chord clears the way for more passenger trains to be run on the main line.

TODMORDEN CURVE   17 May 2015

The £8.8 million reopening of the 500-metre Todmorden curve in May 2015 enabled a new direct train service to be introduced between Blackburn and Manchester. The 10-year project, a partnership between Northern Rail, Network Rail, Lancashire County Council and Burnley Council, put Burnley and Accrington within commuting distance of Manchester.

Picture: Network Rail

TODMORDEN CURVE: A special was one of the first trains to use the reinstated curve

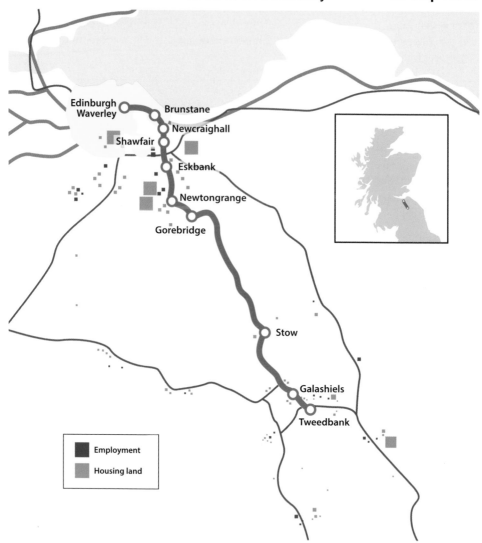

BORDERS RAILWAY: The new line has already boosted the economy in the area

Scotland made headlines throughout the world when the Queen reopened the 48km Borders Railway from Edinburgh Waverley to Tweedbank in September 2015, followed by a series of steam-hauled specials on the line. The £294 million new line reuses part of the former Waverley line that was closed by Labour transport minister Richard Marsh in 1969, six years after its proposed closure in the Beeching report, although the first few kilometres south of Edinburgh survived as a freight route and reopened to passengers

HEAVY WORK: A single line section is laid, above, and a works train delivers ballast on a double track section. Single track sections have created operating problems

in 2002 as part of Edinburgh Crossrail services, with new stations at Brunstane and Newcraighall.

The closure consultation process was dubious. Scots were shocked by the cavalier attitude of the Labour government, and councils in the north of England choosing not to get involved. Financial arguments trumped the wider economic assessments, and ignored the cost of putting more traffic on the roads.

The Borders Railway serves 200,000 people in the Scottish Borders and Midlothian. Apart from HS1 from London to the Channel Tunnel, it is the longest rail line to be built in Britain for over 100 years. With 1.4 million single journeys a year predicted, the Scottish Parliament approved the scheme in 2006, although the benefit to cost ratio was only 1.35:1. It came as no surprise to Railfuture that ScotRail could not cope when the number of prospective passengers was double the official projections. More than 350,000 people used the line in the first three months, against a total of 647,000 expected over the entire year.

Nevertheless, in spite of its shortcomings, the reopening has been hailed a success. Local businesses reported soaring takings, and the historic home of Sir Walter Scott at Abbotsford had to extend its opening hours.

According to the the Scottish Tourism Economic Assessment Monitor, the new line has led to a 27% increase in the number of bed and breakfast visitors to the Borders area, a 20% increase in visitor spending on food and drink, and an

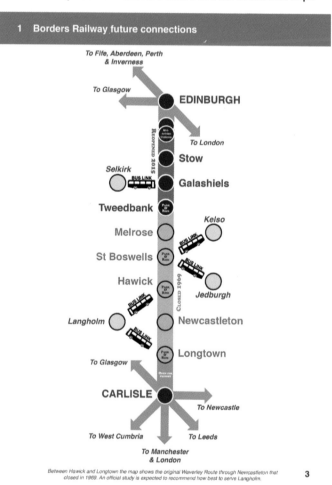

1 Borders Railway future connections

To Fife, Aberdeen, Perth & Inverness

To Glasgow

EDINBURGH

To London

Stow

Selkirk

Galashiels

Tweedbank

Kelso

Melrose

St Boswells

Hawick

Jedburgh

Langholm

Newcastleton

Longtown

To Glasgow

CARLISLE

To Newcastle

To West Cumbria   To Leeds

To Manchester & London

Between Hawick and Longtown the map shows the original Waverley Route through Newcastleton that closed in 1969. An official study is expected to recommend how best to serve Langholm.

3

ON TO CARLISLE: The Campaign for Borders Rail wants to extend the rebuilt line on to Hawick and Carlisle, recreating the old Waverley route which closed in 1969

8% increase in employment related to tourism. The line is used both by commuters to Edinburgh from the Borders, and in the opposite direction by tourists, prompting a campaign to extend it from its current terminus at Tweedbank first to Hawick, and then on to Carlisle and the West Coast main line. The Campaign for Borders Rail published its 20-page *Summary Case for a New Cross-Border Rail Link* in May 2017 arguing that the extension would provide a strategic new link to the national network.

More than 1,000 people worked on the Borders Railway project, repairing or rebuilding 137 bridges, building seven new stations, and re-laying track and sleepers through Midlothian and the Scottish Borders. The line has been criticised for including long stretches of single line, but there are three dynamic loops and the singling has allowed some curves to be smoothed out, allowing higher speeds.

However, rail campaigners believe that the planning methodology was short-sighted, outdated and discredited, so the original concept was downgraded, and the line built with too many capacity restraints. The result has been poor punctuality figures and many train cancellations, exacerbated by a shortage of rolling stock. According to author David Spaven: "The fundamental flaws of a penny-wise, pound-foolish approach to rail reopening will take a lot of money – and a long time – to sort out", but Scotland's Infrastructure

Picture: ScotRail

MADGE ELLIOTT MBE: One of the campaigners who fought for the reopening, hand-delivered a petition to the prime minister in 1968 and finally takes a train on the new line in 2015

Picture: Ray King

ANN GLEN: Author Ann on one of the inaugural trains. She too campaigned for years to get the line reopened. She was a speaker at Railfuture's 2016 conference in Newtongrange

129

Secretary Keith Brown took a different view: "The Borders Railway has become a symbol of this golden age of Scotland's railway, and it will be the vehicle for a new prosperity for the communities on the route." Experts concede that the specification for the line was "descoped" because no private contractor was prepared to build the line as originally conceived at a cost acceptable to Scottish Government. Network Rail took responsibility for construction. Neither ScotRail nor Network Rail can really be blamed for any shortcomings. We now have the railway, though it will be expensive to incease capacity for the long term.

BICESTER-OXFORD PARKWAY   26 Oct 2015

About 16km of existing line was completely rebuilt from Oxford Parkway to Bicester, where a new 1km chord (near Gavray Drive) connected it to Chiltern Railways' main line from London Marylebone to Birmingham. The new stretch of line has changed from a 60kph single track line into a 160kph double track line. Islip station was rebuilt as was Bicester Town station, which was renamed Bicester Village when it reopened in 2015. The extensive work enabled a half-hourly London Marylebone to Oxford Parkway timetable to be introduced in October 2015. It was a major event for Chiltern Railways and for Britain. Prime Minister David Cameron opened the line at the new Oxford Parkway station (on the A34 road near Kidlington), from where, until the extension into Oxford opened in December 2016 (see Oxford Parkway-Oxford below), a park-and-ride bus took passengers into the city centre. It was dubbed the Evergreen 3 project.

Picture: Ray King

BICESTER CURVE: A train from London Paddington heading towards Oxford on the new 1km chord at Bicester which was part of Chiltern Railways' Evergreen 3 project

Although most people were in favour of the new line, a number of local protests and other planning difficulties meant the project took 21 years to complete. Chiltern Railways invested £130 million of the £320 million cost.

The service considerably enhances the prospects for East West Rail, and the line now forms the first phase of East West Rail which should eventually extend from Oxford to Bletchley, Bedford, Cambridge and East Anglia, although the review of the Network Rail investment programme in 2015 has delayed reopening from Bicester to Bletchley by four years.

See also Bicester Village and Islip in Chapter 2
See also Chapter 5: Lines opening soon, East West Rail

348,886
TONNES OF BUILDING MATERIALS DELIVERED FOR NEW ROADS AND OVER BRIDGES

ONE TWO
NEW STATION HAS BEEN BUILT AND ONE COMPLETELY REBUILT

60,505
TONNES OF RECYCLED BALLAST WAS USED TO BUILD THE NEW LINE

OVER 7,000
GREAT CRESTED NEWTS RELOCATED

OVER 6,500
PEOPLE WORKED ON THE PROJECT

FOUR
NEW ROAD BRIDGES HAVE BEEN BUILT AND ONE ROAD BRIDGE HAS BEEN REBUILT AND IMPROVED

36
LEVEL CROSSINGS HAVE BEEN REPLACED OR REMOVED

TEN
ARTIFICIAL BADGER SETS CONSTRUCTED

60 NEW SIGNALS HAVE BEEN INSTALLED

EIGHT NEW FOOTBRIDGES HAVE BEEN BUILT

3,853
METRES OF 39 FOOT DEEP GROUND SUPPORTS TO STRENGTHEN FOUNDATIONS ALONG THE LINE

11 MILES OF EXISTING LINE HAS BEEN REBUILT

TWO
TEMPORARY SWALLOW SHELTERS INSTALLED

A Chiltern Railways graphic illustrating some of the complexity of the Evergreen 3 project

---

YEOVIL JUNCTION-YEOVIL PEN MILL   Dec 2015

This line remained technically open for passenger trains only for booked diversions, but a regular service, Mondays to Fridays and summer Saturdays, was introduced by South West Trains from 14 December 2015, including through services to and from London Waterloo.

NORTON BRIDGE CHORD   29 Mar 2016

Network Rail built 10km of new railway near Norton Bridge, Staffordshire, over a two-year period to deal with one of the last major bottlenecks on the West Coast main line, deemed a project of national significance.

Four rivers had to be diverted and new bridges built to carry the railway over roads. The new section of line allows trains travelling to the Manchester area from the West Midlands to travel over, rather than across, existing tracks from the south to Crewe and Scotland.

The new route starts near Great Bridgeford and runs slightly west of the main line. It then swings eastward on the new flyover near the Norton Bridge junction to join the route to Stoke-on-Trent.

The Government is proposing a permanent closure of Norton Bridge station, which has been out of use since 2004, and served only by a rail replacement bus service.

OXFORD PARKWAY-OXFORD   11 Dec 2016

After a series of planning challenges, the 6km section from the new Oxford Parkway station into the existing Oxford station finally opened on 11 December 2016. Chiltern Railways had to invent a lighting system to warn bats in Wolvercote tunnel of an approaching train, provide alternative homes for badgers, and protect a colony of great crested newts. Humans (allotment holders) also fought a rearguard action to defend their right to push wheelbarrows over the rail line.

From Oxford station, London trains can now head north to reach Marylebone via Bicester, or south via the GWR route to Didcot and London Paddington. At a Railfuture conference in Oxford in 2013, Chiltern's project engineer Stephen Barker explained the challenges of the Evergreen 3 project, and outlined how the East West Rail Consortium plans to extend the line to Bedford and beyond. Oxford's then Lord Mayor Delia Sinclair said the rail projects would see Oxford regain its position as a global gateway, although, as late as 2016, the city council was backing some North Oxford residents in their demand for "silent" track, even though Network Rail had installed noise barriers.
See also Chapter 5: Lines opening soon, East West Rail

WOLVERCOTE TUNNEL: Chiltern Railways had to invent a lighting system to warn bats when a train was coming into the tunnel

CORFE CASTLE: A South West Trains class 159 diesel unit about to leave Corfe Castle (Swanage Railway) for Bournemouth (National Rail) with a special train in 2013

SWANAGE   13 Jun 2017

A project to restore and upgrade 6km of former Network Rail line to allow passenger trains on the preserved Swanage Railway to connect with the national rail network at Wareham was completed in 2017, a year late. Regular trains began running in June 2017, relinking Swanage and Wareham by rail after a break of 45 years. More than 1,000 wooden sleepers were replaced, half a mile of track laid, a quarter-mile-long embankment given a major upgrade, and undergrowth and drainage cleared along 9km of embankments and a new set of points installed at Furzebrook. Swanage Railway has blazed a trail here and credit is due to them for the way their staff and volunteers have steadily worked through and resolved the issues that have arisen. The Swanage Railway has set a trend which may be followed around Britain. Two examples are Alnmouth-Alnwick and Taunton-Minehead and the North Norfolk Railway at Sheringham.

See also Chapter 9: The shape of things to come

MANCHESTER'S GREAT LEAP FORWARD: The new Ordsall chord under construction, above in June 2016, and below in February 2017. It is part of the ambitious Northern Hub project to stimulate economic growth. Improved services are expected to go as far as Newcastle and Hull in the east, and Chester and Liverpool in the west

Chapter 5

Lines opening soon

ORDSALL CHORD, MANCHESTER   2017

Major improvements to rail services in Manchester and across northern England will be possible once the 300 metres of the new Ordsall chord are completed in December 2017. New direct links to Manchester Airport from across the north of England will become possible, congestion at Manchester Piccadilly will reduce by a quarter, with some services being rerouted through Manchester Victoria, and the three main Manchester stations, Victoria, Oxford Road and Piccadilly will be linked.

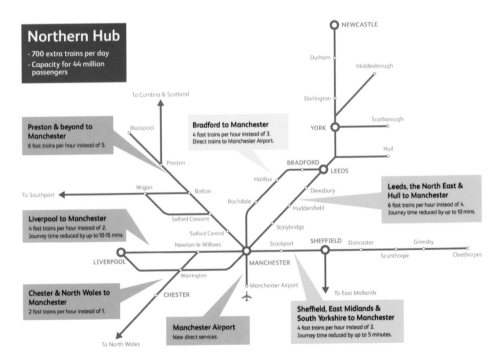

NORTHERN HUB: This map of the wide-ranging planned improvements was published in 2013. The then Chancellor George Osborne visited in 2014, unveiling a plaque at Manchester Airport station marking the start of work on the Hub

Picture: M R Site Services

THAMESLINK 2013: The solar-panelled roof of Blackfriars station can be seen in the foreground of this picture five years before the completion of the Thameslink programme in 2018. By clearing the way for more trains through the centre of London, the Thameslink scheme is expected to make a major contribution to reducing the pollution caused by London's road traffic. Top left in the picture is the City of London, one of the worst pollution hotspots in Europe

The current £6.5 billion project is a major extension to the existing Thameslink north-south route through central London. It will involve 168 stations, many of which will be able to accommodate new class 700 12-coach trains. The project involves the complete reconstruction of London Bridge station, the creation of two additional tracks on a  viaduct between the western end of the platforms and Metropolitan junction, with one new station at Farringdon and another at Blackfriars spanning the Thames with entrances on both sides of the river. A new Bermondsey dive-under was brought into use over Christmas 2016. The so-called Canal Tunnels that once served platforms 12-14 at King's Cross have been rebuilt, and opened to service trains on the existing Thameslink branch to gain access to the new Hornsey maintenance depot. Passenger services on this route should start in May 2018, once the rebuild of London Bridge is complete, and will create many new journey opportunities. Semi-

Picture: Network Rail

THE PAST: London Bridge in 2010 with the Shard partly built and the station roof still intact over the station's terminal platforms

Picture: Network Rail

THE FUTURE: An artist's impression of London Bridge station, adjoining the Shard, with Tower Bridge in the foreground

fast services from Cambridge North to Brighton and from Peterborough to Horsham will run via Gatwick Airport and connect at Farringdon with Crossrail (and thus London Heathrow Airport). There will also be a stopping service to Maidstone East. Semi-automatic operation will enable up to 24 trains per hour through the core in the peak by the end of 2018.

The original Thameslink route was created in 1988 by reopening (as advocated by

Railfuture and at the instigation of the former Greater London Council) a 2.5km section of line from Blackfriars to Farringdon, used by freight trains until 1970 but which closed to passengers 70 years earlier. This enabled through services across central London from Brighton and Gatwick Airport to St Albans, Luton and Bedford, and has been a resounding success. However, there were pathing problems at London Bridge and no spare capacity at peak periods.

See also Chapter 4: New lines for passengers, Hitchin flyover

LONDON CROSSRAIL (Elizabeth line)   Expected 2018

Tunnelling is complete on Europe's biggest construction project, the £16 billion London Crossrail, and work on fitting out the railway was well under way in 2017. The project is over 80% complete and more than 50% of the track has been laid. New British-built Bombardier Aventra trains are being delivered for Crossrail (now called the Elizabeth line) and are being introduced on London Liverpool Street-Shenfield services until the tunnels open. The first trains are seven carriages and 160 metres long, to fit existing platforms at Liverpool Street. Nine-car, 200 metre-long trains, which can carry up to 1,500 people, will be introduced from May 2018 between Heathrow and Paddington and will run along the

Picture: Crossrail

STEPNEY GREEN: This is the crucial place where Crossrail divides, with one branch going east to Stratford and Shenfield and the other going south east to Woolwich and Abbey Wood. In June 2017 workers were fitting the cabling

LIMMO PENINSULA: One of the extensive Crossrail work sites, where the river Lea meets the Thames. It is bathed in artificial light, just like the Millennium Dome, now renamed the O2 Arena, on the south side of the Thames. In 2013, when this picture was taken, two boring machines were lowered into a deep shaft at Limmo so they could start tunelling twin bores towards Canary Wharf and central London

FARRINGDON: Women working on Crossrail join the then Rail Minister Claire Perry (the only woman not in high-viz working gear in this picture) in 2016. She praised Crossrail for helping to make construction an attractive career for women, who make up nearly a third of the workforce compared to a rail industry average of 16%

entire route in 2019. It will link Kent and Essex to Heathrow Airport. In June 2009, Prime Minister Gordon Brown and Mayor of London Boris Johnson marked the start of construction when the first steel piles were driven for the new Canary Wharf Crossrail station. Crossrail has involved the construction of 42 kilometres of new railway tunnels and a further 14 kilometres of station and interchange tunnels. It goes under the centre of London to link the Great Eastern line at Liverpool Street to the Great Western at Paddington. Crossrail is the biggest transport infrastructure project in Britain since the authorisation of the Channel Tunnel rail link. Overhead electric wires are also being extended from Airport junction near Hayes so Crossrail trains can go to Reading. First mentioned on a 1943 London County Council map and formally proposed by a government study in 1989, the scheme was promoted in the early 1990s but rejected by Parliament in 1994. City of London and government support led to its revival a decade later. Two main line stations will serve London's West End (at Tottenham Court Road and Bond Street). Crossrail is also a way of releasing capacity on the London Underground.

Operating an all-stations service on the slow lines from Paddington and the main line from Liverpool Street, the 24 trains per hour on the core section will provide considerable additional capacity across central London, and could carry 200 million passengers a year. Crossrail will run 137km, as far west as Reading, but not as far east as Ebbsfleet, which was suggested in the Superlink scheme. Reading is already the second

PADDINGTON: Crossrail's new station box was being created below street level, to the left of the existing station, in this 2013 picture. Eastbourne Terrace was closed to road traffic for a year to make way for Crossrail's construction machinery

busiest station outside London after Birmingham New Street and has been remodelled at a cost of £500 million to reduce bottlenecks and increase capacity. Some critics complain that future capacity has been restricted by limiting station platforms to 10 coaches and building tunnels too small for double-deck trains such as those used on the Paris RER network.

The cost is being split three ways between the Government, London businesses (partly through a 25-year two-pence supplementary increase in business rates) and fare revenues.

In 2007, despite parliamentary powers not yet being conferred, the Government confirmed the financing just days after funding from the City of London Corporation, Canary Wharf Group and Heathrow Airport owner BAA was agreed. Developer Berkeley Homes promised £160 million towards a station at Abbey Wood.

Work on the site of the £1 billion combined Underground and Crossrail interchange at Tottenham Court Road started in 2009. Tunnel construction began in 2010. Transport for London will own the line through the tunnel rather than Network Rail, but NR will be the infrastructure manager. The line will be integrated into TfL's existing zonal fare system and Oyster smartcard system. A premium fare will operate between Hayes and Heathrow. In 2009 the Government announced it would protect the route of a potential future Crossrail extension from Abbey Wood to Gravesend, Kent.

Crossrail is exceptional in providing so many new interchanges. Former Tube stations at Tottenham Court Road, Bond Street and Whitechapel have been comprehensively rebuilt to accommodate Crossrail passengers. Farringdon and Paddington, which already had connections between Tube and National Rail, have also undergone massive engineering work. The DLR station at Custom House now has an adjoining Crossrail station. Network Rail has built a new station at Abbey Wood to accommodate Crossail and North Kent services.

LAVERTON-BROADWAY   2018

The Gloucestershire and Warwickshire Railway is rebuilding its preserved line from Laverton to a new station at Broadway, the jewel of the Cotswolds. The volunteer-run railway already operates 19km of line between Cheltenham Racecourse and Laverton, five kilometres south of Broadway. The railway's president Pete Waterman OBE spearheaded a successful campaign to raise £1.25 million. It aims to rebuild the railway from Laverton to Broadway by 2018 and in the future to extend as far north as Honeybourne, which is on the National Rail network. Railfuture has supported plans for relaying 10 kilometres of track from Stratford-upon-Avon to reach Long Marston and reconnect with Honeybourne station, which was reopened in 1981. This would open up the possibility of National Rail trains sharing the volunteer-run railway and running from Birmingham to Cheltenham where the line could theoretically be extended to the National Rail station of Cheltenham Spa. The Stratford-Honeybourne section was the subject of a 2012 business study by Arup who considered that the reinstatement was perfectly feasible, at a cost of £60 million for mainly single line, and would be viable with a cost benefit ratio of 2.03. Railfuture contributed nearly half the cost of a JMP Consultants report in 2010. Planning permission has been granted for the reopening

of the line from Honeybourne to Stratford-upon-Avon with a new station at Long Marston. Reopening Stratford-Honeybourne would require Ministerial approval of a Transport & Works Act order. National rail services could run over the Gloucestershire & Warwickshire line only with its permission. While the former rail route is blocked by a road in Cheltenham, and is a popular walk and cycleway, the possibility remains of ultimately making a connection just south of Cheltenham station to reinstate a rail route between Birmingham and Cheltenham via Stratford.
See also Chapter 3: Stations opening soon, Broadway

HALTON CURVE   2018

Passenger trains were effectively withdrawn from the 2.7km Halton curve in 1975 and it almost closed completely in 2004 but work this year will clear the way for a passenger service. The curve scheme is bringing back into full use the section of the line that links the Chester-Warrington line and the Liverpool-Crewe line at Frodsham junction. North Cheshire Rail Users believe it could reopen to passenger operation by 2018. £10 million was allocated to the curve as part of the Liverpool City Region Growth Deal. Upgrades to track and signalling on the curve will enable a new hourly service, in both directions, between Liverpool and Chester, serving Liverpool Lime Street, Liverpool South Parkway (for Liverpool John Lennon Airport) Runcorn, Frodsham and Helsby.

PORTISHEAD LINE   Expected 2019 or 2020

Reopening for passengers the 14km line from Bristol Parson Street junction to Portishead, which closed in 1964, could cost £58 million and is part of the MetroWest Phase 1 project, overseen by the West of England Partnership. A new site has been found for a Portishead station, and Pill station will be reopened. The line to Portbury Dock reopened for freight trains in 2002 at a cost of £21 million but to run a service to a new station at Portishead would require rebuilding 4.5km of track from Portbury Dock junction. The reopening of the line is considered a Nationally Significant Infrastructure Project under the Planning Act 2008 and requires a Development Control Order.

FILTON ABBEY WOOD-HENBURY   2020

Reopening the 4km line from Filton Abbey Wood to Henbury for passengers is part of Phase 2 of the Metro West project, estimated to cost £43 million and expected to be completed in 2020. The sponsors, the West of England Partnership and the local enterprise partnership have proposed initially that Henbury should be served by a spur from Filton to keep the rolling stock costs down and make the scheme affordable. Local groups are however campaigning for the complete loop as far as St Andrews Road to be restored with a circular service back to Bristol via Clifton Down. They argue that new housebuilding in the area will justify the full loop.

TAVISTOCK-BERE ALSTON   2020

Sponsored by Devon County Council, this 9.6km extension of the Tamar Valley line from Bere Alston would provide a link to the nearest big town at Tavistock, which has been without a railway since 1968. The estimated cost of £33 million includes a station just south of the town and would be part-funded by a new housing development. It would provide faster journeys to Plymouth than the very congested road and would provide better access to Dartmoor for tourists. It would also be a valuable step towards closing the gap to Meldon to complete a second route between Plymouth and Exeter via Okehampton. At present, Plymouth is the only town in England of its size with only one rail connection to the national network, and one that is vulnerable to periodic storm damage at Dawlish.

Picture: Ray King

MELDON VIADUCT: This could take Okehampton passengers to Plymouth

CROXLEY LINK   Expected after 2020

The Croxley rail link is designed to link the Metropolitan line into London Overground at Watford High Street and the West Coast main line at Watford Junction.
The 2016 draft Hertfordshire County Council Rail Strategy also mooted a diesel service

between Watford Junction and Milton Keynes via Aylesbury, with a connection to Oxford via East-West Rail at Winslow. Two new stations are planned on the Croxley Link, Cassiobridge (in Ascot Road) and Watford Vicarage Road (serving both Watford Stadium and the general hospital. The current Watford Metropolitan station will be used only for stabling. A Transport and Works Act Order for the project was issued in 2013, and in a parliamentary answer in December 2016, a budget of £284 million was mentioned. Construction should have started in 2015 and be finished by 2018 but there is no obvious progress being made and the 2020 completion date looks unrealistic, as only initial work has been undertaken. Costs doubled as the county council added more enhancements to its wish list. Rail campaigners were alarmed when the scheme was omitted from Transport for London's 2016 business plan. By mid 2017 there seemed to be a funding gap of £50 million about which Conservative Transport Secretary Chris Grayling and Labour London Mayor Sadiq Kahn are unlikely to agree. The *Borehamwood & Elstree Times* reported in March 2017 that a spokesperson for the mayor of London had said: "This project is outside London and therefore responsibility for delivering it ultimately lies with the Government. Transport for London is happy to discuss with the Government how this funding gap can be filled, but, as this scheme is outside London, it is not right that London taxpayers should have to pay even more towards it." £130 million of taxpayers' money has already been spent on the project.

BARKING RIVERSIDE LINK   2021

A £263 million 4km extension of the Gospel Oak to Barking railway line to Barking Riverside, with a new station on the site of the former Barking power station (closed 1981) has been approved and will serve 10,800 homes. It is Britain's largest brownfield

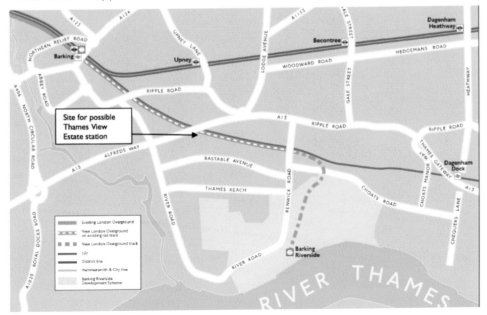

regeneration scheme and £172 million is coming from developers Barking Riverside Ltd for the rail extension. There will be 1.6 km of new track, a spur off the line from Barking to Tilbury and passive provision will be made for a future intermediate station to be added. In early 2017 the Government had shortlisted three companies as possible builders of the line and its authorisation as a Transport and Works Act scheme, allowing work to begin later that year, with services starting in 2021.

Electrification of the existing Gospel Oak line was completed in 2017 and new four-car electric trains will enter service in 2018. Campaigners would like to see a further extension from Barking Riverside, across the River Thames via a future Belvedere crossing to a station in Thamesmead, and then on to Abbey Wood to connect with the future Crossrail line.

In a 2015 public consultation, 90% of respondents were in favour of the extension. Former London Mayor Ken Livingstone had planned to extend the Docklands Light Railway from Gallions Reach with proposed stops in Beckton Riverside, Creekmouth, Barking Riverside, Goresbrooke, and Dagenham Dock, but the plan was abandoned in 2008. The promise of the Overground, however, has given new life to the regeneration project although local rail users say there should be another station on the extension, at Thames View Estate.

Railfuture believes that another rail crossing of the Thames in east London is necessary, allowing trains from Brighton and Gatwick to serve Canary Wharf direct and then proceed to Stansted airport.

ASHINGTON LINE   Expected 2021

Picture: Trevor Watson

PUBLICITY: Flying Scotsman on the Ashington, Blyth and Tyne line in 2016

In 2015 Northumberland County Council agreed to fund a Network Rail GRIP2 feasibility study into restoring passenger services on the freight line between Newcastle and Ashington, with intermediate stations at Northumberland Park (Metro Connection), Seghill, Seaton Delaval, Newsham for Blyth, Bebside and Bedlington. The South East Northumberland Users Group is campaigning to reopen the line by 2021, with a direct route to Newcastle Central and replace the existing Metro line with its 13 intermediate stations.

EAST WEST RAIL   2022-2025

In November 2016, Chancellor of the Exchequer Philip Hammond announced £110 million of funding for the Bicester-Bedford segment of East West Rail to be opened by 2025. In December 2016, the Government set up a new "special purpose vehicle", independent of Network Rail, to design, build and operate East West Rail. Rob Brighouse, the former managing director of Chiltern Railways, was appointed chairman, while Phil Verster was made managing director. Mr Verster was MD of ScotRail when the Borders Railway reopened in 2015.

Network Rail included EWR in its plans for 2014-2019 but a reappraisal by its new chairman Sir Peter Hendy envisaged a delay of between three and seven years. However, in 2016 the National Infrastructure Commission designated a rail link between Oxford and Cambridge as a "once in a lifetime opportunity" to foster development of towns along the corridor such as Bicester, Milton Keynes and Bedford, and not just an economic benefit.

Chiltern Railways kickstarted East West Rail by reopening the section from Bicester to Oxford in two stages, from December 2015 to December 2016. Phase 2 of the project will reopen the disused line from Bicester to Bletchley, where it will link into the existing Marston Vale line into Bedford. Trains could also run between Milton Keynes and London Marylebone via Aylesbury. The design includes a new station at Winslow

DERELICT, BUT NOT FOR LONG: The former Oxford-Bletchley line at Steeple Claydon was derelict, left, in 2016. Rail campaigner Paul Krebs sits on the platform of the old Winslow station, right. This will be transformed into the 160kph East West Rail link and close by, High Speed Two's north-south line will be built

(planning permission granted by Aylesbury Vale District Council in June 2017), two new platforms at Bletchley, 18 new bridges, 22 new footbridges or subways and changes to 97 railway crossings. Railfuture agrees with consultants Jacobs that so many benefits have been identified that the delay in building EWR is costing the economy over £1 million per week. There is also a campaign to reinstate a Bedford-Northampton service, both for passenger trains and to provide a link between Felixstowe and the freight terminal at Nuneaton.

EWR is divided into three sections: Oxford-Bedford (western), Bedford-Cambridge (central) and Cambridge to Norwich, Felixstowe and Ipswich (eastern). The decision on which route EWR should take between Bedford and Cambridge is critical. If it crosses the East Coast main line near Tempsford, it could lead to the development of a new town with 7,000 homes on the old Royal Air Force airfield site and a new interchange station, close the the A1 road.

See also Chapter 4: New lines for passengers, Bicester-Oxford

See also Chapter 4: New lines for passengers, Oxford Parkway-Oxford

WISBECH-MARCH   Expected 2024

The reopening for passengers of the 12km March to Wisbech line is backed by Cambridgeshire County Council and the Greater Cambridge Greater Peterborough

Local Enterprise Partnership which has agreed to pay £3.3 million for a Network Rail GRIP 3 study. The reopening could cost up to £75 million but the Government is said to be keen to implement it as a demonstrator for other rail reinstatements which might involve another "special vehicle", independent of Network Rail, to deliver the project. To date some £336,812 has been spent on studies and consultations.

HEATHROW WESTERN LINK   Expected 2024

Network Rail is planning to build a new £500 million rail link to allow trains from the Great Western line near Langley to gain access to Heathrow airport, by tunnelling five kilometres from near Langley to Terminal 5. Rail passengers should then be able to travel to the airport from Reading, Twyford, Maidenhead and Slough without going into London Paddington. Public consultation was carried out in 2016 with 81% support for the scheme. Building is planned to start in 2019 and the service should be running by 2024. The scheme has been promoted by Thames Valley Berkshire local enterprise partnership. There should be four trains per hour between Reading and Heathrow.

GLASGOW AIRPORT RAIL LINK   Expected 2025

Plans were resurrected in October 2016 by Renfrewshire and Glasgow City Council to create a rail link to Glasgow Airport. The new idea is a tram-train operation, using existing rail to Paisley Gilmour Street and on-street running to the airport. The £144 million plan, with grants from the UK and Scottish governments, is aiming for an opening in 2025 with four trains an hour off peak but reduced frequency during rush hours.
In September 2009 the Scottish Government cancelled the proposed Glasgow Airport Rail Link because of budget cuts. GARL had been expected to open in time for the 2014 Commonwealth Games, as a nationally significant project, with a four-trains-per-hour service.

HIGH SPEED TWO   Expected 2026-2033

Despite orchestrated opposition in the media, Parliament approved High Speed Two which will link London, Birmingham, the East Midlands, Leeds, Sheffield and Manchester. The latest cost estimate for the project is £24 billion. The second reading of the enabling Bill was passed in 2014 with 452 MPs in favour and 41 against. The Bill received royal assent in 2017. It will be completed more than 20 years after Britain's first high speed line from London to the Channel Tunnel. HS2 is to be built in a Y configuration, with London at the bottom, Birmingham at the centre, Manchester top left, and Leeds top right. Work on the first leg is scheduled to begin in 2017, reaching Birmingham by 2026, Crewe by 2027, and be completed by 2033. The first phase will provide services to Scotland via a combination of HS2 and the existing West Coast main line. In January 2017, the Government embarked on a £2.75 billion acquisition process to design, build and maintain a fleet of 60 trains capable of 360 kph.
Railfuture has campaigned for high speed services to be integrated into the existing rail network, and for the terminus at London Euston to link into the HS1 terminus at

St Pancras. A terminus is also planned at Birmingham Curzon Street, with a new high speed interchange station at Solihull near the National Exhibition Centre. There will also be a Manchester Interchange station at Manchester Airport.
In January 2017, HS2 Ltd revealed eight possible station sites, including three in Doncaster for parkway stations.

HEATHROW AIRTRACK Staines to Heathrow   Uncertain

Airtrack was an eminently sensible scheme to connect Heathrow's Terminal 5 to London Waterloo, Reading and Guildford with some Heathrow Express services being extended to Staines. There was to be a new tunnel from Terminal 5 to Stanwell Moor, a new line across the moor, and a chord at Staines. BAA announced it was abandoning the project in April 2011 when Transport Secretary Philip Hammond (Chancellor of the Exchequer in 2017) questioned whether trains should have priority over motorists at level crossings in his constituency of Egham. Although railway managers were surprised by his attitude, it did highlight one of the problems of Airtrack – level crossings which would have been in constant use and for which there is no easy bridging alternative. In October 2011 Wandsworth Council announced a revised plan called Airtrack-Lite. Hounslow Council suggested a link via Bedfont in 2016.

Pictures: HS2

HS2: The Government awarded contracts in July 2017 worth £6.6 billion to build High Speed Two between London and Bimingham. Construction work is expected to begin in 2018 on tunnels, embankments and viaducts

Chapter 6

Metro, light rail and tramways

Tyne and Wear Metro   1980

Running mostly on former British Rail tracks, a new era of light rail in the UK was ushered in by the first phase of the Tyne and Wear Metro. Construction work began in 1974 with Phase 1 opened to the public in 1980.

Trains were extended to South Shields in 1984 and to Newcastle Airport in 1991. In 2002 the Metro was extended to Sunderland, sharing the station platforms and tracks with heavy rail trains, and terminating on a rebuilt route at South Hylton. Three new stations also opened in Sunderland – Park Lane, Stadium of Light and University. With the opening of the Sunderland extension, Metro became the first in Britain to use track shared with main line trains, between Pelaw and Sunderland.

The newest Metro station is £3.2 million Simonside, which opened in 2008, giving the system a total of 39 new stations and 21 former BR stations converted for Metro use. The 2015-16 annual ridership figure for the Metro system as a whole was over 40 million. A complete ban on cycle carriage makes it difficult for green transport campaigners to be sympathetic to the system, and families without a car can be severely disadvantaged as a result. The Metro is publicly owned but operations were contracted out to DB Regio until March 2017 when they were taken back in-house.

Docklands Light Railway   1987

The DLR, also known as the Regeneration Railway, opened in 1987 at a cost of £77 million with just 15 stations. It now serves 45 stations and carried 116.9 million passengers in 2015-16. The original 12km system consisted of two main routes, intersecting at Poplar. There were terminals at Tower Gateway, Stratford and Island Gardens. It was followed by extensions, west to Bank in 1991, east to Beckton in 1994, under the Thames to Greenwich and Lewisham in 1999, and to King George V dock via London City airport in 2005. The network had stretched to more than 32km with 38 stations. Three months after the opening of the link to London City Airport around 70,000 passengers a week were using it, above projected levels. More passengers arrive at the airport by public transport than at any other airport in the UK.

A £180 million 2.5km extension from King George V station in twin tunnels under the Thames to Woolwich Arsenal was started in March 2006 and completed on time in July 2007. It opened in January 2009. A £238 million 6km route from Stratford International to Canning Town with new stations at Abbey Road and Star Lane opened in August

2011 and also provided a link from Stratford International station to the existing Stratford regional station. The DLR followed the route of the former North London Line from Stratford to Canning Town, which closed in December 2006 for conversion. A second platform was provided at Stratford regional station to cope with demand. The DLR enabled passengers to get to the 2012 Olympic site from City airport without changing trains. Former NLL platforms at Canning Town, West Ham and Stratford were converted to DLR operation.

Transport for London launched a consultation in 2007 for an extension of the Beckton line 6km eastwards, through new tunnels and along raised viaducts, to Dagenham Dock from a new junction at Gallions Reach, with possible new stations at Beckton Riverside, Creekmouth, Barking Riverside, Dagenham Vale and Dagenham Dock but this scheme has been superseded by an extension of the London Overground Gospel Oak-Barking service along a new spur off the Tilbury line to a station at Barking Riverside.

Much of the DLR system is on viaducts that are up to 160 years old. Without any level crossings, it uses driverless trains on all routes, with maximum frequency achieved by its moving-block signalling system. Patronage has continually grown, train lengths have been increased, platforms extended and new intermediate stations have also been opened, including Langdon Park (December 2007) on the Canary Wharf-Stratford line, which cost £7.5 million and was funded by the Government's community initiative fund and Leaside Regeneration.

London Underground   since 1960

The London Tube system has been developing since the Metropolitan Railway, the world's first underground line, opened in 1863. This ran in shallow cut-and-cover tunnels, and trains were steam hauled. Indeed, steam did not disappear from Met line service until 1960, when the Rickmansworth-Amersham and Chesham section was electrified. Steam locos were uncoupled and replaced by electric locos at Rickmansworth. North of Harrow-on-the-Hill, the line is shared with Chiltern Rail services into Marylebone. The first deep-tube Central London Railway opened in 1900. There are now 11 Underground lines which include some surface running. In 2015-16, the London Underground carried 1.34 billion passengers.

The Victoria line opened in 1968-71 and has 21km of line with 16 stations. The Jubilee line opened in 1979, taking over the Stanmore branch from the Bakerloo line with a new tunnel section between Baker Street and Charing Cross. The Jubilee line was extended in 1999 from Green Park station through Docklands to Stratford, resulting in the closure of the short section of tunnel between Green Park and Charing Cross. The Jubilee line is now 22.5km long and has 27 stations.

A new Wood Lane Tube station opened in 2008 to serve the Circle and Hammersmith & City lines. An earlier Wood Lane station, on the Central line, closed in 1947. What remained of the station was redeveloped for the Westfield shopping centre which opened in 2008.

London Underground Northern line to Battersea 2020

Construction has started on the £1billion extension of the London Underground Northern line from Kennington to Battersea via Nine Elms. Two new 3.2km tunnels were being bored in 2017 and two new stations will be built at Nine Elms and Battersea. Expected to open in 2020, the project is being funded entirely through contributions from Battersea Power Station and other developers of flats, although the European Investment Bank also agreed to provide a £480 million loan. The project is the first addition to the Tube network since the Jubilee line extension which opened in 1999 and was crucial in making the Canary Wharf development successful.

London Underground Bakerloo line to Lewisham 2029

Consultations were held in 2017 on the proposed Bakerloo line extension from Elephant & Castle to Lewisham, with two stations in Old Kent Road and one in New Cross Gate. Later extensions could take the Bakerloo to Hayes and/or Bromley. It is anticipated that Transport for London will submit a Transport & Works Order application in 2019. Estimated opening date for the extension to Lewisham is 2029 and costs are estimated to be £3.1 billion.

Glasgow Subway

Glasgow's Subway opened in 1896 with a track gauge of four feet (1,219mm). It is 10.5km long with 15 stations. It has never been expanded in 120 years, although since 2010 it has undergone a £290 million upgrade. Railfuture has campaigned for the Glasgow Crossrail project which, if approved, would involve the Subway's West Street station being redeveloped as an interchange to the main line Crossrail. Subway patronage was 13 million in 2014-15.

Manchester Metrolink 1992

Greater Manchester's Metrolink is the most extensive light rail system in Britain and is made up of seven lines radiating from Manchester city centre to Altrincham, Ashton-under-Lyne, Bury, East Didsbury, Eccles, Manchester Airport and Rochdale. The Metrolink system has 92 stops along 96km of standard-gauge track, which makes it the largest light rail system in Britain. There is a mixture of on-street track shared with other traffic, segregated sections and converted former rail lines. It is operated by a fleet of Bombardier Flexity Swift trams.

Phase 1 opened in stages during 1992 from Bury to Altrincham. It was created by the conversion of two former British Rail electrified commuter lines, linked up by a short stretch of on-street running from Manchester Victoria to Manchester Central conference centre (the site of the former Manchester Central station), with a spur from Piccadilly Gardens to Manchester Piccadilly station.

Phase 2 runs from Cornbrook via the redeveloped Salford Quays to Eccles, and was opened in 2000. From 2011, it also served MediaCityUK at Salford Quays, where the BBC opened new headquarters.

Phase 3a saw a 23km extension from Manchester Victoria via Oldham to Rochdale open in 2013, replacing the former rail line. Nine stations, Dean Lane, Failsworth, Hollinwood, Oldham Werneth, Oldham Mumps, Derker, Shaw & Crompton, New Hey and Milnrow were converted, and six new tram stops added at Monsall, Central Park, South Chadderton, Freehold, Kingsway Business Park and Newbold.

A 3.9km extension from Droylsden to Ashton-under-Lyne opened in 2014, a 4.3km extension from St Werburgh's Road to Didsbury opened in 2013, and a new 14 km line to Manchester Airport opened in 2014. The sections through Oldham and Rochdale were also modified to allow street running through the town centres.

Work on a £165 million second city crossing to link Manchester Central conference centre with Manchester Victoria station opened in February 2017.

Next comes the 5.5km line from the Eccles route through Trafford Park to the Trafford Centre shopping mall, for which a Transport and Works Act Order was granted in October 2016. Currently costed at £350 million, the line is due to open in 2021, with intermediate stops at Wharfside (close to the Manchester United football ground), Imperial War Museum, Village, Parkway and EventCity. Enabling work started in January 2017.

Sheffield Supertram   1994

The 29km network opened in stages between 1994 and 1995 and is owned by South Yorkshire Passenger Transport Executive, while the trams are operated and maintained by Stagecoach, which offers integrated ticketing with its bus operations.

A tram-train extension to Rotherham is currently under construction and is scheduled to open in 2018 after many delays. It is intended as a pilot for future British tram-train operations. Trams from Sheffield city centre will head along the present Supertram Meadowhall route to Tinsley, then run on Network Rail's line through Rotherham Central station to the Parkgate shopping centre.

The route will be electrified to 750V dc but the trams can also be equipped for 25kV ac to take advantage of any future electrification of the main line section.

Midland Metro (Birmingham and Wolverhampton)   1999

The number of people using the Midland Metro rose to record levels in 2016 after the tram system was extended on to the streets of Birmingham city centre. Midland Metro opened in 1999 but the network is expected to triple in size by 2027 thanks to a £1.2 billion expansion plan. Phase 1 runs mostly via the little-used former Great Western main line between Birmingham Snow Hill and Wolverhampton, with on-street running for the last kilometre into Wolverhampton. The route was chosen because it was the easiest to deliver, but consequently misses the most built-up catchments, while duplicating existing rail services for the first 5km. So patronage levels in 2015-16 were 4.8 million, nowhere near the 18 million predicted, although it still provides a useful connection to places between the two cities and is important in encouraging regeneration within the corridor. Happily much support from local government is reflected in a programme of extensions which should make the network much more attractive to passengers. Railfuture staged its November 2016 conference in Birmingham to celebrate the opening of the Metro extension to New Street station. A further extension, to be built between 2017 and 2019, will continue from New Street station for 800 metres to Victoria Square and Centenary Square. Because this section passes Birmingham's impressive civic buildings, the city council has insisted on wire-free operation, and it is intended to run the 800 metres on battery power.

Two more extensions were approved by the Department for Transport in 2016, and will take advantage of battery power to save the cost of erecting wires at locations where overhead clearances are problematic. A link from the present Wolverhampton terminus at St Georges to a new transport interchange at Wolverhampton station is expected to open by 2019. Work on the diversion of utilities has started.

In Birmingham a 1.3km extension to Edgbaston via Broad Street and Hagley Road should open by 2021, at which time it is planned to run a service of 10 trams per hour between Edgbaston and Wolverhampton.

Following an application for a Transport and Works Act Order in October 2016, work is expected to start in 2019 on a £137 million extension to Digbeth, which would serve the existing city centre rail stations and the proposed HS2 station at Curzon Street. This extension should open in 2023.

In early 2017, work began on the 11km disused line from Wednesbury to Brierley Hill to clear vegetation. Construction work is expected to get under way in 2019 with the aim of getting the route (with some deviations for street running) back into use for a Metro tram service by 2023.

The Midland Metro Alliance, a partnership of nine organisations that aims to "transform the West Midlands by delivering the best integrated transport system for the future" came into effect in 2016 with the ambitious remit to expand the Midland Metro network.

Croydon Tramlink   2000

This 28km three-line network opened in May 2000 and cost around £200 million, £125 million from the Government and £75 million coming from the private sector. It included former rail routes and some on-street running. The network has four lines from central Croydon, with eastern termini at Beckenham Junction, Elmers End and New Addington, and a western terminus at Wimbledon, where there is an interchange with London Underground and main line services.

Originally owned by Tramtrack Croydon Ltd as a 99-year design, build, operate and maintain concession, the network was sold in summer 2008 for £98 million, and the network is now run by Transport for London. This allowed TfL to increase the frequency of trams in the off-peak period and purchase more vehicles. Tram operations have been the responsibility of FirstGroup since day one. Congestion in the centre of Croydon should be relieved in 2021 by the construction of the £12 million Dingwall Road loop, west of East Croydon station, but long-awaited links to Sutton and to Crystal Palace are unfortunately nowhere to be seen in TfL's immediate plans.

Nottingham Express Transit 2004

The first section of the NET opened in 2004, having cost £200 million. 14km long, with 4km of street running, Line One was a success from the start, and within four years usage had exceeded the most optimistic forecasts. This route runs from Hucknall beside the Worksop-Nottingham railway as far as Wilkinson Street depot, then it takes to the streets through Hyson Green and past the Forest (site of the famous Goose Fair), serving the centre of Nottingham before reaching

A Phoenix Park-bound tram in Nottingham centre

Nottingham station. There is a short branch to Phoenix Park, a business area, which also has a large car park. The success of Line One prompted the construction of two extensions from Nottingham station, both opened in August 2015. The 7.6km line to Clifton South, a south-western suburb of the city, runs along the old Great Central's Manchester-Marylebone main line for 1.6km south of Wilford. The 9.8km line runs west past the Queen's Medical Centre and Nottingham University, then through Beeston and Clifton to Toton Lane. The terminus of each new line has toilets, ticket machines, a coffee kiosk, secure cycle storage, bus interchange and large car parks.

Since December 2011 the network has been the responsibility of the Tramlink Nottingham consortium, the trams being operated by a consortium of Keolis and Wellglade, owners of the local Trent Barton bus company. A wide range of available tickets includes day tickets for all the city's public transport and special offers include event tickets, giving reduced fares to sports matches, concerts and theatrical performances. A number of extensions to the NET system have been envisaged, the most extensive of which would give Nottingham a city-wide network. In addition a report for Nottingham and Broxtowe councils in 2015 raised hopes of a 6km extension of the Phoenix Park line under the M1 then through Kimberley to the Giltbrook Retail Park, at a cost very tentatively estimated at around £150 million. There was also the possibility that this line could be extended through Eastwood and Heanor to Ripley.

Edinburgh 2014

The £776 million 14 km-long 15-stop tramline from Edinburgh Airport through the city centre to York Place finally opened on 31 May 2014, curtailed, several years late and dramatically over budget. A public inquiry under Lord Hardie was still investigating in 2017 how the scheme had gone wrong. However, in the first full calendar year of operation there were 5.1 million journeys, exceeding the targets set in the business model. The latest development of the line saw the opening of the Edinburgh Gateway interchange with ScotRail train services in December 2016. Edinburgh City Council is planning to extend the line from the city centre 5km, along the originally approved route to Leith Newhaven.

Edinburgh Trams have agreed with ScotRail that if the rail network is disrupted, ticket holders will be able to travel on the tram network free of charge. Railfuture would like to see such an arrangement on every tram system in Britain, so it is very unfortunate that the nearest tram stop is not more convenient for passengers arriving at Edinburgh Waverley station.

Blackpool tram extension to Blackpool North   2019

Following the successful modernisation of its Blackpool-Fleetwood tramway in 2012, Blackpool Council has applied to the Secretary of State for powers under the Transport and Works Act to construct and operate an extension that closed in 1936 from North Pier to Blackpool North national rail station. In 2014 the council agreed to contribute towards the £21 million cost, and aims to open the line by April 2019.

Proposed tram schemes

In the late 1990s, 25 new tram schemes were envisaged. Sadly only Edinburgh survived a Government change of heart. Proposed schemes in Leeds, Bristol, South Hampshire and Liverpool were all abandoned by the Department for Transport because of its unwillingness to fund the shortfall between the business case and the actual cost, even though each had gained Transport and Works Act approval. In an age of concern about the pollution caused by diesel exhausts, there is a growing realisation that trams are vastly superior to buses and guided busways, as is shown by the general popularity of the lines that have opened. Many local authorities are keen to see their introduction.

UK modern tram systems

Name	Opened	Stops	Length
Tyne & Wear Metro	Aug 1980	60	78km
DLR	Jul 1987	45	38km
Manchester Metrolink	Apr 1992	92	96km
Sheffield Supertram	Mar 1994	48	29km
Midland Metro	May 1999	26	21km
Croydon Tramlink	May 2000	39	28km
Nottingham NET	Mar 2004	50	32km
Edinburgh	May 2014	15	14km
Blackpool (modernised)	Apr 2012	39	18km

Tram-train

It is possible that at least some of the branch lines closed at the time of the Beeching axe could have been saved if they had been converted to light rail or tram-train operation.

Belatedly the idea of allowing trams to access the main line, which has been successful in Germany, is now being tried out in Britain.

See Sheffield Supertram section earlier in this chapter.
See Chapter 5: Lines opening soon, Glasgow Airport rail link

If the tram-train concept had been implemented in Britain earlier, they would have provided much better service than the busways that the Department for Transport has promoted: Fareham-Gosport, Luton-Dunstable and Cambridge-St Ives.

The current Sheffield-Rotherham tram-train pilot, expected to be completed in 2018, will be critical for future tram-train projects. The tram-train vehicles built for this are dual-voltage. In Kassel, Germany, the vehicles are hybrid electro-diesel.

For Britain, it may be necessary to have a hybrid electro-diesel version of tram-train for running on non-electrified sections of line.

The Penistone line tram-train project (shelved in favour of Sheffield-Rotherham) would probably have required a hybrid electro-diesel vehicle.

Railfuture is opposed to the Abbey Line (Watford to St Albans Abbey) being converted to tram-train operation, but there could be advantages if a diversion to Napsbury and street running allowed tram-trains to gain access to St Albans City station (avoiding the present trek up Holywell Hill).

In South Wales, there have been suggestions that tram-trains could form part of the area-wide Metro.

Tram-train was also considered as an option to run along part of the Robin Hood line north of Nottingham, and beyond Ruddington south of the city on to the former Great Central line towards Loughborough and Leicester.

In the West Midlands, extensions of the Metro light rail network have taken precedence in Wolverhampton and Birmingham city centres, but the mothballed former rail alignment from Wednesbury had been earmarked for tram-train use.

In Greater Manchester and Cheshire, the former Cheshire Lines route towards Chester via Knutsford and Northwich was also at one stage being considered for tram-train operation as an extension beyond Altrincham. It remains to be seen if Transport for the North will re-consider the plan.

Chapter 7

Ireland

NORTHERN IRELAND

Unlike the rest of the UK, the bus and rail networks in Northern Ireland are totally integrated and run by state-owned Translink. As well as building new link lines and some reopening, Translink has invested in a new fleet of diesel multiple units and ridership is on the increase. The most significant rail developments have been in Belfast, where three termini – Great Victoria Street, York Road and Queen's Quay – once served the Dublin, Larne and Bangor routes respectively, while a cross-city Belfast central railway linking the Dublin and Bangor routes fell into disuse. Until the 1980s the lines to Coleraine, Portrush and Londonderry also ran from York Road, but were re-routed into Great Victoria Street via the line from Antrim to Lisburn, with four intermediate stations reopened, to integrate these services better into the rest of the network. York Road then served only the line to Larne Harbour, for ferries to Scotland.

The Belfast Central Railway route was rebuilt, with new stations at Belfast Central and Botanic (April 1976) and later City Hospital, and both Great Victoria Street and Queen's Quay were closed. All services except that to Larne were re-routed into the new Belfast Central station, (albeit less central than Great Victoria Street). In 1994 a new 2km line was built across the Lagan estuary, enabling Larne trains to reach Belfast Central, and Yorkgate station replaced the adjacent York Road terminus on what was now a through line. In due course, services to the north-west reverted to the direct route to Belfast Central via Yorkgate, leaving the Lisburn-Antrim line with a minimal service of three daily trains, now withdrawn.

Finally, Great Victoria Street terminus was rebuilt and reopened with a triangular junction enabling commuter services to regain this more convenient terminus adjacent to the re-invigorated city centre, hotels and bus station. This new improvement and the cross-harbour link were supported by European Regional Development funding. Additional platforms as part of the proposed rebuilding of Great Victoria Street may allow the Dublin-Belfast Enterprise service to return to its traditional terminus.

In 2001, 24km of track was reopened, from Bleach Green to Antrim. Level crossings were upgraded, a new signalling system installed and bridges repaired. Stations were opened at Mossley West and Templepatrick with 75% of the £16.5 million funding coming from the European Regional Development Fund. This reduced the journey time to Belfast for passengers from Antrim and all stations to the north and west by about 20 minutes, leading to an immediate 29% increase in passengers according to Translink. Full services were introduced on 1 July 2001. Since this reopening, the Antrim-Lisburn line via Crumlin is no longer used by passenger trains, although it is maintained for emergency use. It offers a route that is only 2km from Belfast International Airport.

Other station openings or reopenings include Newry, Poyntzpass, Scarva, Cullybackey, Bellarena, Dhu Varren and University. Crumlin, Glenavy and Ballinderry also reopened in the 1970s but closed again in 2003.

In 2014, a Northern Ireland Executive 20-year strategy document proposed an expansion of the rail network by reopening of the 32km Antrim-Knockmore/Lisburn line, mothballed in 2003, together with a new rail link to Belfast International Airport at Aldergrove. Other potential candidates for reopening identified in the report include Antrim-Castledawson and the lines from Portadown to Armagh and Dungannon.

Another positive development is the Translink plan to double the frequency of the service between Derry and Belfast in 2017 to hourly, following a £42 million upgrade of the Derry-Coleraine line.

Bellarena station was resited across the road in 2016, with a passing loop that works better than the one it replaced at Castlerock.

REPUBLIC OF IRELAND

Ireland has undergone a railway revival with both planned and actual reopening of routes and stations, and a comprehensive fleet renewal programme. The process started in the 1980s with the Dublin Area Rapid Transit project, a heavy-rail line under the heart of the capital that links the Heuston and Connolly termini in a similar manner to Crossrail in London. The DART proved to be a major success, and electrification of Dublin's core north-south suburban route between Howth and Bray was then extended north to Portmarnock and Malahide and south to Greystones, with many stations reopened, and new ones built at Grand Canal Dock, Clontarf Road and Clongriffin.

In November 2016, after a 13-year campaign led by Rail Users Ireland and following city centre signalling and platform improvements, a new service between Newbridge and Grand Canal Dock provided for the first time in a more than a century a direct commuter link between the two halves of the Irish railway network. The combination of the Phoenix Park Tunnel and Luas Cross City works will finally result in a joined-up rail network in Dublin.

A new terminal station was built in the Dublin Docklands area, which will relieve the pressure that increased commuter trips have brought to the Dublin Connolly main line and DART station. The southern end of the long-closed Navan line out to the dormitory town of Dunboyne has been rebuilt, and extended to a major new park-and-ride facility located on the M3 motorway.

With the success of the DART project, Iarnród Éireann invested in a fleet of modern diesel multiple units to extend and upgrade the Dublin suburban services on the main lines radiating from the capital. Services to Kildare on the Cork line, Mullingar and Longford on the Sligo line, and Drogheda/Dundalk on the Belfast line were the first to be improved and some new, or seriously improved, stations were introduced at

LIMERICK: The west of Ireland is accessible by rail from Dublin. However the reopening of the Western Rail Corridor to Claremorris and Sligo has stalled

locations where major development had taken place. However, further development has been scaled back, with work not expected to start until 2020.

Substantial investment has also taken place in new track and rolling stock. Jointed rail is now very much the exception and all inter-city carriages are less than 13 years old. The refurbished original DART units are the oldest passenger stock at 31 years, with most commuter stock being much newer. This investment, however, came at the expense of structures and signalling, with collapses to viaducts at Cahir and Malahide, a roof at Cork Station and several cuttings.

At the start of the new millennium, the Irish Government Transport 21 plan envisaged major investment in transport infrastructure. In particular, there has been a concerted effort to improve bridges and ballast to enable higher speeds on the main Dublin-Cork line, improvements that will also help journeys on other routes. Plans included new stations and further improvements to the capital's suburban services. As well as the Cork route upgrade, the commuter service from Dublin Heuston to Kildare has had special treatment, with additional tracks, new stations such as Adamstown, and others being completely rebuilt. Away from Dublin, rail and station reopenings have taken place in a number of locations. The long-standing suburban service from Cork to Cobh was supplemented by local trains running out to Mallow on the Dublin line. In July

2009 the line to Midleton, on the former Youghal branch, which closed in 1963, was reopened with an intermediate station at Carrigtwohill, at a cost of €75 million.

Following the earlier reinstatement of services between Limerick and Ennis, services from Ennis to Athenry were reinstated in 2010, allowing for a Limerick to Galway service. This involved the total reconstruction of some 57km of track, new signalling, and new stations at Sixmilebridge, Gort, Ardrahan and Oranmore. Reopening the remainder of the Western Rail Corridor to Claremorris and Sligo has however stalled, because of poor passenger numbers on the first section.

Back in Dublin, much of the Bray to Dublin Harcourt Street route, closed in 1958, was reconstructed as the Green Line of the popular Luas light rail operation, which opened in 2004. The core network of this efficient system that adds on-street running to parts of old rail and canal alignments, was extended in 2010. An extension of the line south from Sandyford to serve another new commercial and residential development at Cherrywood was opened in 2010, while construction of a link to the Red Line, and continuation north to Broombridge began in 2013. Work is well progressed and services are expected to begin in December 2017.

A Red Line extension was opened in 2009 from the city centre east to serve the mushrooming developments in the Docklands area of the city. In 2011, it was again extended west from a new junction at Belgard to the new Citywest suburb.

Although it has full planning approval, Metro North – rebranded as New Metro North – a light rail underground line running out from the city centre north to Dublin airport and the commuter town of Swords, has an uncertain future because of a lack of commitment to the large capital cost.

In early 2017, the National Transport Authority was consulting on the future make-up and strategy for rail transport in Ireland. After consulting Rail Users Ireland, Railfuture objected to two of the suggested closure proposals, as they have international significance as ferry links.

Chapter 8

Beyond the Channel

Elsewhere in Europe, many line reopenings have taken place and new lines have been built while other key routes have been upgraded and many new metro or light rail schemes opened. The concept of tram-train has been developed in urban areas.

Rail transport is seen as a practical solution to the challenges of global warming and climate change, by reducing dependence on the private car. In March 2011, the European Union's White Paper on Transport said rail should become the main mode of transport for journeys up to 600km by 2050.

In January 2014, the EU launched a new transport infrastructure policy, TEN-T, with a budget of €24.05 billion up to 2020. TEN-T aims to close the gaps between member states' transport networks, remove bottlenecks and overcome technical barriers by harmonising standards. It promotes and strengthens seamless transport chains for passengers and freight, while keeping up with the latest technological trends. A second generation of work plans approved in December 2016 establishes the basis for action until 2030.

The high speed rail routes developed in France from 1981 are well known. In July 2017, two new high speed lines linking Paris to Bordeaux (from Tours) and Rennes were inaugurated. France was an example to countries such as Spain and Germany, while Italy, Belgium and the Netherlands have also linked major cities by stretches of new line. Long stretches of high speed line have enabled rail to compete with air and improve its market share, and this effect has also been seen in Italy between Turin, Milan, Rome and Naples.

Switzerland and Austria have built short sections of high-speed line and/or new tunnels to increase capacity as well as reduce travel time between cities. The Westbahn from Vienna to Innsbruck via Salzburg has been upgraded by new tunnels and cut-offs, and new tunnels have also improved access to city centres, such as at Malmo, Antwerp and Leipzig.

Stations on new lines are sometimes built in open country to serve the park-and-ride market (les gares des betteraves or "beetroot stations" as our French colleagues call them). Such stations should always have good public transport access.

In more heavily populated countries such as Germany, the new lines sometimes form strategic links, with high speed trains passing seamlessly between the new and classic routes.

In France, however, away from the TGV routes, cross-country services are generally poor, with infrequent trains and unattractive journey times. Rail freight has shrunk dramatically. Many local lines have closed or been replaced by bus services, although this trend is being reversed where responsibility for local lines has been transferred to *departements*, together with generous funding for reinvestment.

All but three cities in France had closed their tram networks by the beginning of the 1960s. However, from the 1980s the French government actively encouraged and partly funded the construction of new tram lines and metros, with the result that over 20 cities, such as Grenoble, Strasbourg, Rheims, Nantes, Montpellier, Bordeaux and Angers reintroduced the tram, sometimes on reserved track, while others such as Lille, Toulouse and Lyon built new metros.

The train-tram concept was developed in Mulhouse, to give commuters easier access to the city centre, building on the success of similar schemes at Karlsruhe and Saarbrucken in Germany.

In Berlin, reunification led to many rail links abandoned in 1961 being restored but also to the creation of a facility which the city had never had before – a central station.

Responsibility for local trains in Germany has largely been transferred to the *lande*, with funding for improvements to infrastructure and trains, and this has generally resulted in more frequent and better used services. Increasingly, these services are being franchised, although many have been retained by DB which is allowed to bid for them.

Few European countries have seen the steady and sustained growth in passenger numbers evident in Britain over the past 20 years.

A new bridge and tunnel opened across the Oresund in 2000, linking Copenhagen and its airport to Malmo in Sweden, and providing Norway and Sweden with direct rail access to the rest of mainland Europe. It was already possible to travel by train from Copenhagen to Hamburg via the Great Belt Link, but proposals for a further fixed link across the Fehmarn Sound will considerably shorten the journey time between Denmark and Germany.

The political changes since 1989 have led to some modest but significant reopenings of cross-border lines. For example, it is now possible to travel from Vienna to Bratislava by two separate routes, whereas before there was only one. At least three lines have reopened across the Czech-German border and the Polish towns of Swinoujscie and Kostrzyn now have passenger services across the border into Germany. Three lines crossing the German-French border (at Wissembourg, Lauterbourg and east of Mulhouse) now have passenger trains again.

Conversely, the replacement of Yugoslavia by six independent countries, together with war in the 1990s, has resulted in a reduction in through train services, lengthy frontier waits and an end to through trains from western Europe to Greece and Turkey. Some local train services have also been withdrawn.

There remain other instances where there is potential for a restored cross-border service, or indeed where the link has declined or been withdrawn. Sometimes this is because one country's policy on investing in infrastructure or subsidising services is at variance with its neighbour's.

However, 2016 saw the 24km line between Oloron-Sainte-Marie and Bedous reopen after 36 years of closure, to improve access to the Pyrenees national park. The line also forms part of the former international link from Pau (France) to Canfranc in Spain, from where a Spanish diesel train still runs twice daily to Zaragoza. Reopening to Canfranc is now scheduled for 2020.

Portugal is starting work in 2017 to reopen the Guarda-Covilhã section of the Beira Baixa route which will provide a strategic north-south link within Portugal as well as providing a cross-border route into Spain via the frontier crossing at Vilar Formoso. Services should be running again by 2019.

The European Union's Rail Baltica project aims to improve rail links between Estonia, Latvia, Lithuania and Poland, bypassing the Russian outpost of Kaliningrad (the former German city of Königsberg) and prioritising efficient standard gauge links rather than the wider Russian gauge.

Information about rail developments in 20 European countries can be found on the website of the European Passengers' Federation, to which Railfuture is affiliated.

AND BEYOND EUROPE...

Everyone has heard of the impressive Japanese bullet trains which started in 1964 and now cross the entire country. China, South Korea and Taiwan have all built high-speed rail networks. China's high-speed achievements and plans are massive, but the country has also built thousands of kilometres of conventional lines too. China is also helping other countries to expand their railways. In December 2016, land-locked and mountainous Laos celebrated the launch of construction of a 400km long railway from the Chinese border to its capital Vientiane, which is now linked by rail to Thailand. Turkey opened its first high speed line in 2009 and hopes to complete the Istanbul-Ankara section by 2018.

In the USA, the passenger railroads struggle to develop, with limited funding or political encouragement. Service frequencies are low, on some long-distance services not even daily, and equipment on many commuter lines is outdated. On the East Coast, commuter lines continue to meet the needs of the cities they serve, and the North East corridor does support a reasonably frequent and fast service between Washington, New York and Boston, but no high speed lines have yet been constructed in the USA. In the mid west, passenger services are thin, but some cities here and on the West Coast are investing in metro systems, including the use of freight lines. American railroads do, however, have a huge share of the freight market, unlike European railways, and conflicts continue to arise between the capacity requirements of passengers and freight on lines that are mainly owned by freight railroads.

Picture: Borders Railway

SCOTLAND: The busy Edinburgh southern by-pass road was temporarily diverted at Sherriffhall in 2014 to allow a bridge to be constructed for the Borders Railway. Once the bridge was complete, the road was moved back to its original alignment

Picture: Crossrail

LONDON: Huge boring machines have created Crossrail, the new railway for the UK capital. This picture shows the 2014 breakthrough at Victoria Dock

Chapter 9

The shape of things to come

The demand for more station and line reopenings is now overwhelming and this will only increase as demand for rail access continues to grow and many future developments will depend on rail for their success. The capability of the rail industry to meet this demand is inadequate, with a tortuous project development process and no single authority in England having responsibility for sponsoring or coordinating new line proposals.

There has been a transformation in government thinking, responding to public demand, and it is now recognised that reopening closed lines, plus many new stations, can help Britain meet the Government's target to reduce carbon emission levels by 80% by the year 2050 and open new sites for development.

Of course the expenditure of public funds must be fully justified, but Network Rail's Governance for Railway Investment Projects (GRIP) and the need for Development Consent Orders (a requirement of the 2008 Planning Act) have made the process cumbersome, slow and expensive. North of the border, the devolved government's Scottish Transport Appraisal Guidance (STAG) is yet another process that must be negotiated to achieve the same aim.

A proposal from North Somerset Council to reopen the Portishead line had reached GRIP Stage 3 in 2013 when it was subsumed into MetroWest, and the GRIP process had to be restarted from scratch. It is currently back at Stage 3. When the various processes do finally arrive at a benefit/cost ratio (BCR), it is invariably too pessimistic. Reopening the Borders Rail line was assessed at the lower limit of viability, so a cheeseparing design was adopted, but this has proved woefully inadequate to cope with the actual demand.

Another difficulty in reopening lines has been the short-term view taken by many politicians and railway managers. History shows that it is difficult to predict the future with any degree of accuracy, so the sensible strategy is to keep options open. Only with hindsight does the value of a closed line become clear, but too often the land has been sold off to farmers and developers. At the very least closed lines should be made into pedestrian or cycle routes, so that the line could be reopened if needed.

In the past, railway managers were sometimes reluctant to support reopenings, and squandered the massive public enthusiasm, seemingly resentful of voluntary lobbying seeking to assist the case for a bigger and better railway. This has changed with the huge growth in rail demand over the past 20 years, and the inability of the road network to cope.

Ghost stations

Rail campaigners would also like to see progress on providing better services at some existing ghost stations which could serve their community much better. For example, Ascott under Wychwood is in the heart of the village and had thousands of pounds spent on a new platform when the Cotswold line was doubled, but has

167

just one train each way, Mondays-Fridays only. Golf Street, Balmossie and Monifieth have a similar skeleton service. Denton and Reddish South are in the heart of the Manchester suburbs, but have one train a week, one way only. Polesworth has one train a day (Monday-Saturday), one way only, after the footbridge to the eastbound platform was removed for route upgrade works and not replaced. Sudbury & Harrow Road is in a prominent town-centre position on a main road, offering excellent rail/bus interchange, but has just four trains each way daily (Monday-Friday only). The station had an expensive platform rebuild a few years ago as part of line upgrade, but no improvement to its service.

Better late than never

In 2009, the Association of Train Operating Companies produced a 24-page consultation document *Connecting Communities – Expanding Access to the Rail Network* drafted by Chris Austin. Few planners and politicians took much notice of it, but Railfuture did. The document identified 75 towns in England with a population in excess of 15,000 that were no longer rail connected. A short-list of 35 resulted, with 14 places identified as probably having a positive business case.

Chris Austin and Richard Faulkner followed up with *DISCONNECTED – Broken Links in Britain's Rail Policy*, published by OPC in 2015, taking the argument further.

In the same year the social benefits of rail reopenings were highlighted in the 57-page *Rural Reconnections* report by the Campaign to Protect Rural England. It showed how reinstating a rail route from Exeter to Plymouth via Okehampton and Tavistock could help with sustainable development in the South West region generally. Also in 2015, the Conservative Bow Group think-tank's report *Reviving Britain's Railways* recommended earmarking cash for reopening railway lines.

The Rossendale valley in Lancashire was identified in the ATOC document as a very large community off the network, along with the area between Leicester and Burton upon Trent. The Ivanhoe line (Leicester-Burton) could and should have been opened years ago. If all 14 schemes were acted on, a million people would benefit.

The Government's view is that new line and station projects should be driven locally and be integrated with spatial plans for new homes, and business and retail development. In Scotland, Wales, London and other passenger transport executive areas, reopening lines such as Ebbw Vale, Borders Railway and the East London line have been driven more by regeneration than by transport needs, but have been none the less successful for that.

In 2016, a National Infrastructure Commission report cited development of the Oxford-Cambridge corridor as a national priority that could happen only if the East-West Rail project were fully completed. To its credit, the Government reacted positively. The Chancellor set aside £100 million to complete the Oxford-Bedford section by 2025, and a further £10 million to determine the route on to Cambridge, while the Transport Secretary created a new vehicle independent of Network Rail to bring it about.

There is, however, no overall strategy which links these individual initiatives, and so no review of how the largest British conurbations not served by rail might be better connected, and how the routes that have survived can be protected. Capacity is expensive to create and easy to destroy. Funding issues are often a bar to delivering rail projects, even though they offer good value and are often very much cheaper than any alternative road scheme. A fundamental issue is still a lack of understanding of what rail can deliver and a generally negative official attitude towards new rail schemes, in contrast to the apparent ease with which some local politicians are able to press for and secure funding for their favourite road bypass schemes, or just one more stretch of dual-carriageway to "ease a bottleneck".

New runways and airport terminals also appear to receive sympathetic treatment from the Government and media even though they conflict with the official and sensible policy of carbon reduction. New rail lines and stations can help achieve improved accessibility and social cohesion, as well as reducing climate change and road congestion. What are we waiting for?

In August 2016, the Government announced a £20 million fund for new railway stations. This is very welcome, but a drop in the ocean when you hear the clamour from all over the country for line and station reopening.

Highways England has £15 billion to deliver smart motorways with all-lane running, and new motorway-style A roads. Confusing to the public, they will be called expressways, rather than A roads or motorways, but this policy is not supported by the majority of the public who are much more aware of pollution and the hazards of road transport than they were in 1960.

Warnings to people to stay indoors when pollution from traffic is at dangerous levels demonstrates the need for a sensible transport policy.

People know that new roads create new traffic and rarely solve traffic problems, but some right-wing newspapers obsessed by the absurd notion of a war on motorists are still obediently putting out anti-rail propaganda on behalf of the road lobby.

By not forecasting traffic levels accurately, and not taking into account induced traffic, the Government miscalculates the net benefits and costs of a new road. But even if the induced traffic is forecast correctly, it will still cause damaging environmental impacts and extra congestion that make building big new roads pointless.

The most authoritative studies into induced traffic are the 1994 SACTRA report *Trunk Roads and the Generation of Traffic*, and the 2006 report *Beyond Transport Infrastructure* by independent consultants for the Countryside Agency and the Campaign to Protect Rural England. Some politicians do not like to be reminded of these uncomfortable facts.

But for those who have kept up to date with events, a rail link is now the basic building block for sustainable development and regeneration. Even the Treasury recognises that railway investment produces a good economic rate of return in the wider economy. The strategic value of of railways is now recognised after years when the economic, environmental and social value of the railway was not widely accepted.

In 1960, many civil servants in the Treasury wrongly believed that a smaller railway would cost the taxpayer less. They were wrong then, and there is no excuse for such thoughts now. They need to find ways to reopen more stations and more lines to deliver a bigger, better railway. The explosion in personal mobility and the demand to travel cannot be accommodated on the road network alone.

In Scotland and Wales, devolved government agencies can sponsor new lines and stations, but in England the Department for Transport does not see expanding the rail network as part of its role and there is no mechanism for the rail industry itself to take the lead. Thus, there is no official structure to consider the need for new railways, although Transport for London and the passenger transport executives have shown what is possible.

It has also become obvious that encouraging more passengers on to the railway with better services and reasonable fares is a good way to improve the finances of both the railway and the nation. All over Britain, local councillors are demanding that their areas should be reconnected with the rail network, and are puzzled when they are confronted with the proverbial brick wall. Rail campaigners know that even the most sensible scheme is unlikely to happen without years of determined persistence in the face of official negativity.

Even some seasoned rail campaigners thought the reopening of the 90km Carmarthen-Aberystwyth line, estimated at £700 million in 2013, was unrealistic. However, compare that with the cost of upgrading 29 kilometres of the A14 road between Cambridge and Huntingdon, where the Government is happily spending £1.8 billion of taxpayers' money. Meanwhile the campaign by Traws Link Cymru for reopening the Carmarthen-Aberystwyth route is growing, while in North Wales, restoring 16km of track between Caernarfon and Bangor could create a 140km circular route around Snowdonia, including National Rail and heritage lines, which incidentally have much to offer in other parts of Britain.

In April 2017, the Welsh Government said it had selected 12 new railway stations (from a list of 46) which would be subjected to a financial analysis: Cardiff Ely Mill/Victoria Park, Cardiff Newport Road/Rover Way, Cardiff St Mellons, Newport Llanwern, Swansea Cockett, Swansea Landore, St Clears, Deeside Industrial Park/Northern Gateway, North Wrexham, South Wrexham, Llangefni and Bow Street.

Heritage railways have successfully used volunteers to reopen lines and stations, but are mainly seen as tourist attractions. With notable exceptions, such as the Severn Valley Railway, they remain a largely untapped resource for public transport users. This could be remedied with a sensible combination of public subsidy and volunteer enthusiasm.

For example:

WEST SOMERSET RAILWAY (Taunton-Minehead)

The longest heritage railway in England has long been physically connected to the main line network at Norton Fitzwarren, but use of the connection has generally been restricted to special workings, loco/stock movements, ballast trains and occasional freight traffic, with regular services running between Bishops Lydeard (the first station on the branch) and Minehead. The gap between Bishops Lydeard and Taunton is covered by a bus link. Re-establishing regular rail services over the connection into Taunton has always been an aspiration, however, and there are hopes that this will move closer to reality in the next year or two, with Great Western trains running to Bishops Lydeard by 2018. In the meantime, in 2016 it became possible to book through day return tickets to the West Somerset Railway from GWR stations, including the bus link. It is believed that this facility will be extended to period returns in 2017.

EPPING-ONGAR RAILWAY

The nearest preserved line to London currently stops just 100 metres short of its original interchange, the London Underground Central Line station at Epping. Its ultimate aim is to get back into Epping station and establish it once again as a rail-to-rail interchange. This was reflected in the Railway's December 2016 submission to the Epping Forest District Council Local Development Plan in which it urged support for this objective, stressing the significance of the railway to the local visitor economy. It also cited the 2013 Report of the All Party Parliamentary Group on Heritage Railways, which provided evidence that on average every pound spent at a Heritage Railway resulted in £2.71 spent in the wider economy.

CHINNOR & PRINCES RISBOROUGH RAILWAY

After some years of terminating tantalisingly short of Princes Risborough at Thame Junction (where passengers are unable to join or alight), in Spring 2016 Network Rail finally agreed connection rights, enabling the railway to remove the boundary buffer stop and reconnect the track. This was followed by the signing of a track access agreement in June 2016, allowing CPRR trains to run into the station area. 2017 will see much work taking place on rebuilding the branch platform at Princes Risborough and laying track into it to create a proper interchange station.

The success of railways throughout Britain has prompted rail campaigners to up their demands. Those who have long wanted the Uckfield-Lewes line reopened are now keen to show how the line could function as part of a new route linking Brighton, Gatwick, Canary Wharf and Stansted Airport. Call it Thameslink 2 or Brighton Main Line 2, it has massive potential, which in 2016 the Government appeared to be waking up to. Like many other lines, the strategic Buxton/Peak Forest-Matlock line in Derbyshire should have stayed open and could now produce direct access from the quarries in the Buxton area to the East Midlands and East Anglia as well as more direct passenger services between Manchester and the East Midlands. While part of it is a heritage railway, and the remainder is the much-valued Monsal Way, running through a national park, the formation of the line remains in position and could be restored.

Picture: SELRAP

Railfuture has supported the Skipton and East Lancashire Rail Action Partnership (SELRAP) financially in its campaign to get passenger trains running again between stations in North and West Yorkshire via

SELRAP's Derek Jennings (in the green tie) shakes hands with Lancashire County Councillor John Fillis. Also in the picture are, from left, County Councillor Azhar Ali, Pendle Borough Councillor Ian Tweedie, Andy Shackleton and Peter Nowland

Skipton and Colne to the principal towns of East Lancashire, Preston and Blackpool. In early 2017, Transport Scotland was consulting the public on its rail infrastructure strategy for post-2019. In its 35-page consultation document, new routes and stations are key questions, but in the introduction it says: "We are also not seeking views from stakeholders on what they believe to be priority investment schemes, whether proposed upgrades to the existing infrastructure, or new routes or stations."

This suggests that new routes and stations are not what Transport Scotland wanted to hear about, though Railfuture ensured they received such views, whether they liked it or not.

With the success of the Borders Railway, campaigners are looking to extend the line from Tweedbank to Hawick and then to Carlisle. Further north, people are asking why the Buchan lines to Fraserburgh and Peterhead – the two towns furthest from the national rail network – cannot be reopened.

Transform Scotland, the sustainable transport alliance, has urged the Scottish Government to protect the route of the Buchan lines so that the cost of reinstating them at a later date is minimised. The regional transport body, Nestrans, is currently investigating how much it would cost to bring back the railway to Buchan.

Glasgow Crossrail and reopening the 8km Thornton-Levenmouth line should also be contenders, while a short branch to St Andrews would connect a world-class university town and tourist centre with the national network. International golf tournaments attract tens of thousands of visitors by road currently. A link from Edinburgh Airport would attract many American visitors out of their hire cars and on to the railway.

In London, even before Crossrail is completed, Crossrail 2, a £27 billion regional project with national significance, envisages a route connecting South Western suburban services via Wimbledon across the capital to Tottenham Hale and the Lea Valley line in north east London. And Crossrail 3 is supported by Lord Adonis who is chair of the National Infrastructure Commission. When Thameslink was created in 1988 by reinstating 650 metres of track, there was some doubt as to how successful it would be. What followed was an amazing response from the public who proved that seamless cross-London services were extremely popular. It is a shame that Crossrail 2 was not mentioned in the Queen's Speech in 2017.

In 2016, Railfuture produced a list of 10 stations that should be prioritised for building or reopening. Edginswell (Devon), Maghull North (Merseytravel), Marsh Barton (Devon), Warrington West and Worcester Parkway have already been mentioned in *Chapter 3: Stations opening soon,* while Parkgate (Rotherham) should open in 2018 as a tram-train station. Railfuture now wants rapid progress on the remaining four – Addenbrooke's (Cambridge), East Leeds Parkway, Peterlee and Soham (Cambridgeshire).

Train operators have spent money on station development through franchise commitments. The National Stations Improvement Plan and the Access for All fund both provide government funding for stations. As a direct and practical contribution, Railfuture has worked with the Campaign for Better Transport and the Department for Transport to publish a guide to *Expanding the Railways.*

Chapter 10

Station openings by date

In this chapter, we list station openings in chronological order, showing date, station name, area and finally, the Government Office regional code. The table and chart show how many stations have opened in each of the Government Office regions. In 2010, the coalition Government announced it planned to abolish regional government, but the regions continue to be used for administrative and statistical purposes.

EE	Eastern England	. . . .	20	SE	South East	18
EM	East Midlands		33	SW	South West	20
LO	London		29	WA	Wales	56
NE	North East		13	WM	West Midlands . . .	25
NW	North West		53	YH	Yorkshire & Humber	40
SC	Scotland		100			

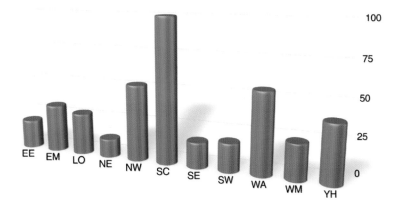

Numbers of stations opened by Government Office regional code.
Some have performed very well while others could try harder

1960   6 stations

07 Nov 1960	GARSCADDEN Glasgow	. . . .	SC
07 Nov 1960	GOLF STREET Angus	. . . .	SC
07 Nov 1960	HYNDLAND Glasgow	. . . .	SC
21 Nov 1960	SOUTHBURY Greater London	. . . .	LO
21 Nov 1960	THEOBALDS GROVE Hertfordshire	. . . .	EE
21 Nov 1960	TURKEY STREET Greater London	. . . .	LO

1961 1 station

06 Mar 1961 ROGART Lairg . . . . SC

1962 1 station

18 Jun 1962 BALMOSSIE Dundee . . . . SC

1965 1 station

14 Jun 1965 DOLGARROG Conwy . . . . WA

1966 3 stations

07 Feb 1966 GARSTON Hertfordshire . . . . EE
01 Apr 1966 SOUTHAMPTON AIRPORT PARKWAY Hampshire . . . . . . SE
27 Jun 1966 LOCHWINNOCH Renfrewshire . . . . SC

1967 4 stations

06 Mar 1967 NEW PUDSEY West Yorkshire . . . . YH
05 Jun 1967 BRANCHTON Inverclyde . . . . SC
05 Jun 1967 DUNLOP East Ayrshire . . . . SC
05 Jun 1967 STEWARTON East Ayrshire . . . . SC

1970 3 stations

05 Jan 1970 NARBOROUGH Leicestershire . . . . EM
04 May 1970 GLAN CONWY Conwy . . . . WA
07 Dec 1970 FALMOUTH TOWN Cornwall . . . . SW

1971 5 stations

01 Feb 1971 KINGSKNOWE Edinburgh . . . . SC
03 May 1971 FENITON Devon . . . . SW
03 Oct 1971 TEES-SIDE AIRPORT Darlington . . . . NE
04 Oct 1971 ALLENS WEST Stockton-on-Tees . . . . NE
06 Dec 1971 NEEDHAM MARKET Suffolk . . . . EE

1972 4 stations

28 Feb 1972 PENALLY Pembrokeshire *Sir Benfro* . . . . WA
01 May 1972 BRISTOL PARKWAY South Gloucestershire . . . . SW
27 May 1972 MATLOCK BATH Derbyshire . . . . EM
21 Aug 1972 SHOTTON Low Level Flintshire *Sir y Fflint* . . . . WA

1973 — 5 stations

05 Jan 1973	BAILDON West Yorkshire	YH
07 May 1973	ALFRETON Derbyshire	EM
07 May 1973	ALNESS Ross and Cromarty	SC
07 May 1973	LLANFAIRPWLL Isle of Anglesey	WA
	Llanfairpwllgwyngyllgogerychwyrndrobwllllantysiliogogogoch Sir Ynys Môn	
23 Jul 1973	STEVENAGE Hertfordshire	EE

1974 — 1 station

25 Nov 1974	BASILDON Essex	EE

1975 — 3 stations

05 May 1975	RUSKINGTON Lincolnshire	EM
05 May 1975	WATLINGTON Norfolk	EE
06 Oct 1975	METHERINGHAM Lincolnshire	EM

1976 — 8 stations

26 Jan 1976	BIRMINGHAM INTERNATIONAL West Midlands	WM
03 May 1976	DUNCRAIG Wester Ross	SC
03 May 1976	GYPSY LANE Redcar and Cleveland	NE
03 May 1976	LYMPSTONE COMMANDO Devon	SW
04 Oct 1976	MUIR OF ORD Ross and Cromarty	SC
04 Oct 1976	PEARTREE Derbyshire	EM
04 Oct 1976	SINFIN CENTRAL Derbyshire	EM
04 Oct 1976	SINFIN NORTH Derbyshire	EM

1977 — 4 stations

02 May 1977	LIVERPOOL CENTRAL Deep Level Merseyside	NW
02 May 1977	MOORFIELDS Merseyside	NW
30 Oct 1977	LIVERPOOL LIME STREET Low Level Merseyside	NW
12 Dec 1977	BRINNINGTON Greater Manchester	NW

1978 — 12 stations

01 Jan 1978	NEWTON AYCLIFFE Durham	NE
03 Jan 1978	AIGBURTH Merseyside	NW
03 Jan 1978	CRESSINGTON Merseyside	NW
03 Jan 1978	GARSTON Merseyside	NW
03 Jan 1978	ST MICHAELS Liverpool	NW
08 May 1978	FIVE WAYS West Midlands	WM
08 May 1978	HATTERSLEY Greater Manchester	NW

08 May 1978	IBM Inverclyde	SC
08 May 1978	LONGBRIDGE West Midlands	WM
08 May 1978	UNIVERSITY West Midlands	WM
23 May 1978	LELANT SALTINGS Cornwall	SW
19 Jun 1978	BRITISH STEEL REDCAR Redcar and Cleveland	NE

1979 — 10 stations

14 May 1979	WEST HAM Low Level Greater London	LO
05 Nov 1979	ANDERSTON Glasgow	SC
05 Nov 1979	ARGYLE STREET Glasgow	SC
05 Nov 1979	BRIDGETON Glasgow	SC
05 Nov 1979	DALMARNOCK Glasgow	SC
05 Nov 1979	EXHIBITION CENTRE Glasgow	SC
05 Nov 1979	GLASGOW CENTRAL Low Level Glasgow	SC
05 Nov 1979	PARTICK *PARTAIG* Glasgow	SC
05 Nov 1979	RUTHERGLEN South Lanarkshire	SC
?? Nov 1979	HEWORTH Tyne and Wear	NE

1980 — 4 stations

12 May 1980	HACKNEY CENTRAL Greater London	LO
12 May 1980	HACKNEY WICK Greater London	LO
15 May 1980	MOULSECOOMB East Sussex	SE
06 Oct 1980	BIRCHWOOD Cheshire	NW

1981 — 5 stations

05 Jan 1981	DRONFIELD Derbyshire	EM
25 May 1981	HONEYBOURNE Worcestershire	WM
24 Jun 1981	NEW HOLLAND Lincolnshire	EM
05 Oct 1981	KENTISH TOWN WEST Greater London	LO
05 Oct 1981	WETHERAL Cumbria	NW

1982 — 9 stations

01 Mar 1982	FITZWILLIAM West Yorkshire	YH
15 Mar 1982	VALLEY Isle of Anglesey *Y FALI Sir Ynys Môn*	WA
22 Mar 1982	BLAENAU FFESTINIOG Gwynedd	WA
26 Apr 1982	DEIGHTON West Yorkshire	YH
15 May 1982	MILTON KEYNES CENTRAL Buckinghamshire	SE
17 May 1982	CROSSFLATTS West Yorkshire	YH
17 May 1982	WATTON-AT-STONE Hertfordshire	EE
04 Dec 1982	WATFORD STADIUM Hertfordshire	EE
13 Dec 1982	SLAITHWAITE West Yorkshire	YH

1983 — 8 stations

16 May 1983	PINHOE Devon	SW
17 May 1983	DALSTON KINGSLAND Greater London	LO
11 Jul 1983	KING'S CROSS THAMESLINK Greater London	LO
12 Sep 1983	BRAMLEY West Yorkshire	YH
03 Oct 1983	CATHAYS Cardiff *Caerdydd*	WA

03 Oct 1983	RUNCORN EAST Cheshire	NW
03 Oct 1983	TEMPLECOMBE Somerset	SW
21 Nov 1983	MOSS SIDE Lancashire	NW

1984   14 stations

10 Apr 1984	SALTAIRE West Yorkshire	YH
12 May 1984	AUCHINLECK East Ayrshire	SC
12 May 1984	KILMAURS East Ayrshire	SC
14 May 1984	BEDFORD ST JOHNS Bedford	EE
14 May 1984	LOSTOCK HALL Lancashire	NW
01 Jul 1984	SOUTH BANK Redcar and Cleveland	NE
09 Jul 1984	SHERBURN-IN-ELMET North Yorkshire	YH
03 Sep 1984	MELTON Suffolk	EE
15 Sep 1984	DYCE Aberdeen	SC
01 Oct 1984	DUNSTON Tyne and Wear	NE
06 Oct 1984	LIVINGSTON SOUTH West Lothian	SC
15 Oct 1984	HUMPHREY PARK Greater Manchester	NW
26 Nov 1984	SILKSTONE COMMON South Yorkshire	YH
1984	SANDWELL & DUDLEY West Midlands	WM

1985   17 stations

25 Mar 1985	MILLS HILL Greater Manchester	NW
01 May 1985	LOCH AWE Argyll and Bute	SC
01 May 1985	SOUTH GYLE Edinburgh	SC
06 May 1985	LOCH EIL OUTWARD BOUND Fort William	SC
13 May 1985	BRIDGE OF ALLAN Stirling	SC
13 May 1985	FLOWERY FIELD Greater Manchester	NW
13 May 1985	HOMERTON Greater London	LO
13 May 1985	LONGBECK Redcar and Cleveland	NE
13 May 1985	MELKSHAM Wiltshire	SW
17 May 1985	PORTLETHEN Aberdeenshire	SC
20 May 1985	ROUGHTON ROAD Norfolk	EE
30 Jun 1985	DUNROBIN CASTLE Sutherland	SC
18 Aug 1985	SMITHY BRIDGE Greater Manchester	NW
30 Aug 1985	DERKER Greater Manchester	NW
30 Sep 1985	BROMBOROUGH RAKE Merseyside	NW
04 Nov 1985	LISVANE & THORNHILL Cardiff *LLYSFAEN Caerdydd*	WA
04 Nov 1985	RYDER BROW Greater Manchester	NW

1986   24 stations

| 24 Mar 1986 | BATHGATE West Lothian | SC |
| 24 Mar 1986 | LIVINGSTON NORTH West Lothian | SC |

24 Mar 1986	UPHALL West Lothian	SC
10 May 1986	SOUTH WIGSTON Leicestershire	EM
12 May 1986	CWMBRAN Torfaen	WA
12 May 1986	LANGLEY MILL Derbyshire	EM
12 May 1986	TELFORD CENTRAL Shropshire	WM
12 May 1986	TIVERTON PARKWAY Devon	SW
12 May 1986	WINNERSH TRIANGLE Berkshire	SE
14 Jul 1986	ARMATHWAITE Cumbria	NW
14 Jul 1986	DENT Cumbria	NW
14 Jul 1986	GARSDALE Cumbria	NW
14 Jul 1986	HORTON-IN-RIBBLESDALE North Yorkshire	YH
14 Jul 1986	KIRKBY STEPHEN Cumbria	NW
14 Jul 1986	LANGWATHBY Cumbria	NW
14 Jul 1986	LAZONBY & KIRKOSWALD Cumbria	NW
29 Sep 1986	BURNLEY MANCHESTER ROAD Lancashire	NW
29 Sep 1986	HALL I'TH'WOOD Greater Manchester	NW
29 Sep 1986	LONDON FIELDS Greater London	LO
29 Sep 1986	WELHAM GREEN Hertfordshire	EE
29 Sep 1986	YNYSWEN Rhondda Cynon Taf	WA
29 Sep 1986	YSTRAD RHONDDA Rhondda Cynon Taf	WA
24 Nov 1986	EASTBROOK Vale of Glamorgan *Bro Morgannwg*	WA
1986	RIBBLEHEAD North Yorkshire	YH

1987 26 stations

19 Jan 1987	ARDROSSAN TOWN North Ayrshire	SC
08 Apr 1987	CLITHEROE Lancashire	NW
13 Apr 1987	BLACKPOOL PLEASURE BEACH Lancashire	NW
13 Apr 1987	CORBY Northamptonshire	EM
29 Apr 1987	TY GLAS Cardiff *Caerdydd*	WA
01 May 1987	EAST GARFORTH West Yorkshire	YH
09 May 1987	BICESTER TOWN Oxfordshire	SE
11 May 1987	HAG FOLD Greater Manchester	NW
11 May 1987	HEYSHAM PORT Lancashire	NW
11 May 1987	LAKE Isle of Wight	SE
11 May 1987	ROTHERHAM CENTRAL South Yorkshire	YH
11 May 1987	SALFORD CRESCENT Greater Manchester	NW
11 May 1987	WESTER HAILES Edinburgh	SC
21 Jun 1987	SUGAR LOAF Powys	WA
27 Jun 1987	CONWY Conwy	WA
03 Aug 1987	METROCENTRE Tyne and Wear	NE
07 Sep 1987	FRIZINGHALL West Yorkshire	YH
28 Sep 1987	BIRMINGHAM MOOR STREET West Midlands	WM
03 Oct 1987	HADDENHAM & THAME PARKWAY Buckinghamshire	SE
04 Oct 1987	DANESCOURT Cardiff *Caerdydd*	WA
04 Oct 1987	FAIRWATER Cardiff *Y TYLLGOED Caerdydd*	WA
04 Oct 1987	NINIAN PARK Cardiff *PARC NINIAN Caerdydd*	WA
05 Oct 1987	BIRMINGHAM SNOW HILL West Midlands	WM
05 Oct 1987	CURRIEHILL Edinburgh	SC

| 02 Nov 1987 | WAUN-GRON PARK Cardiff *PARC WAUN-GRON Caerdydd* . . . | WA |
| 30 Nov 1987 | SANDAL & AGBRIGG West Yorkshire . . . . | YH |

1988   23 stations

21 Apr 1988	CONONLEY North Yorkshire	YH
25 Apr 1988	COTTINGLEY West Yorkshire	YH
14 May 1988	BEDWORTH Warwickshire	WM
16 May 1988	GOLDTHORPE South Yorkshire	YH
16 May 1988	HALEWOOD Merseyside	NW
16 May 1988	LOSTOCK Greater Manchester	NW
16 May 1988	NEWBURY RACECOURSE Berkshire	SE
16 May 1988	THURNSCOE South Yorkshire	YH
20 Jun 1988	FALLS OF CRUACHAN Argyll and Bute	SC
12 Jul 1988	OUTWOOD West Yorkshire	YH
16 Aug 1988	OVERPOOL Cheshire	NW
01 Oct 1988	ARLESEY Bedfordshire	EE
03 Oct 1988	ABERCYNON NORTH Rhondda Cynon Taf *ABERCYNON GOGLEDD*	WA
03 Oct 1988	ABERDARE Rhondda Cynon Taf *ABERDÂR*	WA
03 Oct 1988	CWMBACH Rhondda Cynon Taf	WA
03 Oct 1988	FERNHILL Rhondda Cynon Taf	WA
03 Oct 1988	MARTINS HERON Berkshire	SE
03 Oct 1988	MOUNTAIN ASH Rhondda Cynon Taf *ABERPENNAR*	WA
03 Oct 1988	MUSSELBURGH East Lothian	SC
03 Oct 1988	PENRHIWCEIBER Rhondda Cynon Taf	WA
22 Oct 1988	HOW WOOD Hertfordshire	EE
28 Nov 1988	LICHFIELD TRENT VALLEY High Level Staffordshire	WM
29 Nov 1988	BURLEY PARK West Yorkshire	YH

1989   15 stations

03 Apr 1989	TUTBURY AND HATTON Derbyshire	EM
08 Apr 1989	CANNOCK Staffordshire	WM
08 Apr 1989	HEDNESFORD Staffordshire	WM
08 Apr 1989	LANDYWOOD Staffordshire	WM
17 Apr 1989	BLOXWICH West Midlands	WM
13 May 1989	ISLIP Oxfordshire	SE
15 May 1989	AIRBLES North Lanarkshire	SC
15 May 1989	DRUMGELLOCH North Lanarkshire	SC
15 May 1989	GREENFAULDS North Lanarkshire	SC
15 May 1989	MILLIKEN PARK Renfrewshire	SC
15 May 1989	STEPPS North Lanarkshire	SC
15 May 1989	YATE South Gloucestershire	SW
16 May 1989	DODWORTH South Yorkshire	YH
29 Jul 1989	LLANRWST Conwy	WA
09 Oct 1989	BERRY BROW West Yorkshire	YH

1990   20 stations

| 20 Jan 1990 | RAMSLINE HALT Derbyshire . . . . | EM |

23 Apr 1990	PRIESTHILL & DARNLEY Glasgow	SC
14 May 1990	HEDGE END Hampshire	SE
14 May 1990	SHIELDMUIR North Lanarkshire	SC
14 May 1990	STEETON & SILSDEN West Yorkshire	YH
14 May 1990	SWINTON South Yorkshire	YH
14 May 1990	WHINHILL Inverclyde	SC
29 May 1990	CITY THAMESLINK Greater London	LO
04 Jun 1990	TAME BRIDGE PARKWAY West Midlands	WM
30 Jul 1990	CORKERHILL Glasgow	SC
30 Jul 1990	CROOKSTON Glasgow	SC
30 Jul 1990	DUMBRECK Glasgow	SC
30 Jul 1990	MOSSPARK Glasgow	SC
30 Jul 1990	PAISLEY CANAL Renfrewshire	SC
05 Sep 1990	MEADOWHALL South Yorkshire	YH
10 Sep 1990	WALSDEN West Yorkshire	YH
24 Sep 1990	WORLE Weston-super-Mare	SW
01 Oct 1990	WHISTON Merseyside	NW
01 Oct 1990	WOODSMOOR Greater Manchester	NW
02 Oct 1990	BLOXWICH NORTH West Midlands	WM

1991   5 stations

19 Mar 1991	STANSTED AIRPORT Essex	EE
12 Apr 1991	HAWKHEAD Renfrewshire	SC
13 May 1991	KIRK SANDALL South Yorkshire	YH
27 May 1991	NEW CUMNOCK East Ayrshire	SC
20 Jul 1991	SMALLBROOK JUNCTION Isle of Wight	SE

1992   15 stations

27 Apr 1992	BENTLEY South Yorkshire	YH
11 May 1992	FEATHERSTONE West Yorkshire	YH
11 May 1992	GLENROTHES WITH THORNTON Fife	SC
11 May 1992	PENCOED Bridgend *Pen-y-bont ar Ogwr*	WA
11 May 1992	PONTEFRACT TANSHELF West Yorkshire	YH
11 May 1992	STREETHOUSE West Yorkshire	YH
24 Aug 1992	HORNBEAM PARK North Yorkshire	YH
28 Sep 1992	GARTH Bridgend *Pen-y-bont ar Ogwr*	WA
28 Sep 1992	MAESTEG Bridgend *Pen-y-bont ar Ogwr*	WA
28 Sep 1992	PONTYCLUN Rhondda Cynon Taf	WA
28 Sep 1992	SARN Bridgend *Pen-y-bont ar Ogwr*	WA
28 Sep 1992	TONDU Bridgend *Pen-y-bont ar Ogwr*	WA
26 Oct 1992	MAESTEG EWENNY ROAD Bridgend *Pen-y-bont ar Ogwr*	WA
12 Dec 1992	WILDMILL Bridgend *Y FELIN WYLLT Pen-y-bont ar Ogwr*	WA
21 Dec 1992	WHIFFLET North Lanarkshire	SC

1993   15 stations

08 May 1993	HUCKNALL Nottinghamshire	EM

08 May 1993	NEWSTEAD Nottinghamshire	EM
17 May 1993	MANCHESTER AIRPORT Greater Manchester	NW
20 Sep 1993	GRETNA GREEN Dumfries and Galloway	SC
04 Oct 1993	BAILLIESTON North Lanarkshire	SC
04 Oct 1993	BARGEDDIE North Lanarkshire	SC
04 Oct 1993	CARMYLE Glasgow	SC
04 Oct 1993	KIRKWOOD North Lanarkshire	SC
04 Oct 1993	MOUNT VERNON Glasgow	SC
11 Oct 1993	ADWICK South Yorkshire	YH
03 Dec 1993	ASHFIELD Glasgow	SC
03 Dec 1993	GILSHOCHILL Glasgow	SC
03 Dec 1993	MARYHILL Glasgow	SC
03 Dec 1993	POSSILPARK & PARKHOUSE Glasgow	SC
03 Dec 1993	SUMMERSTON Glasgow	SC

1994   18 stations

27 May 1994	BARROW-UPON-SOAR Leicestershire	EM
27 May 1994	BULWELL Nottinghamshire	EM
27 May 1994	SILEBY Leicestershire	EM
27 May 1994	SYSTON Leicestershire	EM
29 May 1994	CAM & DURSLEY Gloucestershire	SW
29 May 1994	LANGHO Lancashire	NW
29 May 1994	RAMSGREAVE & WILPSHIRE Lancashire	NW
29 May 1994	WHALLEY Lancashire	NW
01 Jun 1994	BRITON FERRY Neath Port Talbot	WA
	LLANSAWEL Castell-nedd Port Talbot	
13 Jun 1994	WALLYFORD East Lothian	SC
27 Jun 1994	LLANSAMLET Swansea *Abertawe*	WA
27 Jun 1994	PYLE Bridgend *Y PIL Pen-y-bont ar Ogwr*	WA
27 Jun 1994	SANQUHAR Dumfries and Galloway	SC
27 Jun 1994	SKEWEN Neath Port Talbot *SGIWEN Castell-nedd Port Talbot*	WA
14 Jul 1994	IVYBRIDGE Devon	SW
05 Sep 1994	PRESTWICK INTERNATIONAL AIRPORT South Ayrshire	SC
27 Sep 1994	CAMELON Falkirk	SC
14 Nov 1994	WATERLOO INTERNATIONAL Greater London	LO

1995   10 stations

24 Sep 1995	THE HAWTHORNS West Midlands	WM
03 Apr 1995	EASTHAM RAKE Wirral, Merseyside	NW
23 May 1995	DIGBY & SOWTON Devon	SW
26 May 1995	WILLINGTON Derbyshire	EM
30 May 1995	CHAFFORD HUNDRED Essex	EE
24 Sep 1995	JEWELLERY QUARTER West Midlands	WM

24 Sep 1995	SMETHWICK GALTON BRIDGE West Midlands	WM
20 Nov 1995	MANSFIELD Nottinghamshire	EM
20 Nov 1995	MANSFIELD WOODHOUSE Nottinghamshire	EM
20 Nov 1995	SUTTON PARKWAY Nottinghamshire	EM

1996   6 stations

08 Jan 1996	ASHFORD INTERNATIONAL Kent	SE
14 Jan 1996	MERTHYR TYDFIL *MERTHYR TUDFUL*	WA
20 Feb 1996	YARM Stockton-on-Tees	NE
11 Mar 1996	FILTON ABBEY WOOD South Gloucestershire	SW
02 Jun 1996	BAGLAN Neath Port Talbot *Castell-nedd Port Talbot*	WA
17 Nov 1996	KIRKBY IN ASHFIELD Nottinghamshire	EM

1997   4 stations

25 May 1997	OKEHAMPTON Devon	SW
01 Jun 1997	ASHCHURCH FOR TEWKESBURY Gloucestershire	SW
01 Jun 1997	RUGELEY TOWN Staffordshire	WM
15 Dec 1997	EUXTON BALSHAW LANE Lancashire	NW

1998   11 stations

09 Mar 1998	BRUNSWICK Merseyside	NW
28 Mar 1998	DALGETY BAY Fife	SC
24 May 1998	CRESWELL Derbyshire	EM
24 May 1998	DRUMFROCHAR Inverclyde	SC
24 May 1998	LANGWITH-WHALEY THORNS Derbyshire	EM
24 May 1998	SHIREBROOK Derbyshire	EM
24 May 1998	WHITWELL Derbyshire	EM
25 May 1998	HEATHROW CENTRAL Greater London	LO
25 May 1998	HEATHROW TERMINAL 4 Greater London	LO
22 Jun 1998	CONWAY PARK Merseyside	NW
23 Nov 1998	WREXHAM CENTRAL Wrexham *WRECSAM CYFFREDINOL Wrecsam*	WA

1999   5 stations

30 May 1999	HORWICH PARKWAY Greater Manchester	NW
30 May 1999	WEST BROMPTON Greater London	LO
30 May 1999	WEST HAM High Level Greater London	LO
08 Sep 1999	BRAINTREE FREEPORT Essex	EE
21 Nov 1999	LUTON AIRPORT PARKWAY Bedfordshire	EE

2000   5 stations

| 26 Jan 2000 | DUNFERMLINE QUEEN MARGARET Fife | SC |
| 28 May 2000 | BRIGHOUSE West Yorkshire | YH |

13 Aug 2000	WAVERTREE TECHNOLOGY PARK Liverpool	NW
17 Sep 2000	LEA GREEN Merseyside	NW
08 Oct 2000	WARWICK PARKWAY Warwickshire	WM

2001 — 1 station

| 12 Mar 2001 | HOWWOOD Renfrewshire | SC |

2002 — 4 stations

15 Apr 2002	BEAULY Inverness	SC
31 Mar 2002	UNIVERSITY Tyne and Wear	NE
03 Jun 2002	BRUNSTANE Edinburgh	SC
03 Jun 2002	NEWCRAIGHALL Edinburgh	SC

2003 — 2 stations

| 19 Oct 2003 | CHANDLER'S FORD Hampshire | SE |
| 04 Dec 2003 | EDINBURGH PARK Edinburgh | SC |

2004 — 1 station

| 21 May 2004 | SAMPFORD COURTENAY Devon | SW |

2005 — 8 stations

21 Feb 2005	GLASSHOUGHTON West Yorkshire	YH
09 May 2005	GARTCOSH Glasgow	SC
12 Jun 2005	LLANTWIT MAJOR Vale of Glamorgan	WA
	LLANILLTUD FAWR Bro Morgannwg	
12 Jun 2005	RHOOSE CARDIFF INTERNATIONAL AIRPORT Vale of Glamorgan	WA
	MAES AWYR RHYNGWLADOL CAERDYDD Y RHWS Bro Morgannwg	
29 Sep 2005	KELVINDALE Glasgow	SC
12 Dec 2005	CHATELHERAULT South Lanarkshire	SC
12 Dec 2005	LARKHALL South Lanarkshire	SC
12 Dec 2005	MERRYTON South Lanarkshire	SC

2006 — 1 station

| 11 Jun 2006 | LIVERPOOL SOUTH PARKWAY Merseyside | NW |

2007 — 5 stations

19 Aug 2007	COLESHILL PARKWAY Warwickshire	WM
14 Nov 2007	LONDON ST PANCRAS International Greater London	LO
19 Nov 2007	EBBSFLEET INTERNATIONAL Kent	LO
09 Dec 2007	LONDON ST PANCRAS International Low Level Greater London	LO
10 Dec 2007	LLANHARAN Rhondda Cynon Taf	WA

2008

06 Feb 2008	EBBW VALE PARKWAY Blaenau Gwent *PARCFFORD GLYN EBWY*	WA
06 Feb 2008	NEWBRIDGE Caerphilly *TRECELYN Caerffili*	WA
06 Feb 2008	RISCA & PONTYMISTER Caerphilly *RHISGA A PHONT-Y-MEISTR Caerffili*	WA
06 Feb 2008	ROGERSTONE Newport *Y TŶ-DU Casnewydd*	WA
27 Mar 2008	HEATHROW TERMINAL 5 Greater London	LO
27 Apr 2008	LLANHILLETH Blaenau Gwent *LLANHILEDD*	WA
19 May 2008	ALLOA Clackmannanshire	SC
03 Jun 2008	MITCHAM EASTFIELDS Greater London	LO
07 Jun 2008	CROSSKEYS Caerphilly *Caerffili*	WA
28 Sep 2008	SHEPHERD'S BUSH Greater London	LO
14 Dec 2008	AYLESBURY VALE PARKWAY Buckinghamshire	SE

2009

26 Jan 2009	EAST MIDLANDS PARKWAY Nottinghamshire	EM
23 Feb 2009	CORBY Northamptonshire	EM
18 May 2009	LAURENCEKIRK Aberdeenshire	SC
27 Sep 2009	IMPERIAL WHARF Greater London	LO
30 Nov 2009	STRATFORD INTERNATIONAL Greater London	LO
30 Nov 2009	WORKINGTON NORTH Cumbria	NW

2010

27 Apr 2010	DALSTON JUNCTION Greater London	LO
27 Apr 2010	HOXTON Greater London	LO
27 Apr 2010	SHOREDITCH HIGH STREET Greater London	LO
27 Apr 2010	HAGGERSTON Greater London	LO
12 Dec 2010	BLACKRIDGE *AN DRUIM DUBH* West Lothian	SC

2011

13 Feb 2011	CALDERCRUIX North Lanarkshire	SC
04 Mar 2011	ARMADALE West Lothian	SC
06 Mar 2011	DRUMGELLOCH North Lanarkshire	SC
18 Jul 2011	SOUTHEND AIRPORT Essex	EE
03 Oct 2011	BUCKSHAW PARKWAY Lancashire	NW

2012

14 May 2012	FISHGUARD AND GOODWICK Pembrokeshire *ABERGWAUN AC WDIG Sir Benfro*	WA

2013 — 3 stations

08 Feb 2013	CONON BRIDGE Ross-shire (Highland Region)	SC
19 May 2013	STRATFORD-UPON-AVON PARKWAY Warwickshire	WM
16 Dec 2013	ENERGLYN & CHURCHILL PARK *ENEU'R-GLYN A PHARC CHURCHILL*	WA

2014 — 3 stations

17 May 2014	JAMES COOK UNIVERSITY HOSPITAL Middlesbrough	NE
01 Sep 2014	LLANDECWYN Gwynedd	WA
14 Dec 2014	PYE CORNER Newport	WA

2015 — 14 stations

17 May 2015	EBBW VALE TOWN *TREF GLYN EBWY* Blaenau Gwent	WA
04 Jun 2015	NEWCOURT Devon	SW
06 Sep 2015	ESKBANK Midlothian	SC
06 Sep 2015	GALASHIELS Selkirkshire	SC
06 Sep 2015	GOREBRIDGE Midlothian	SC
06 Sep 2015	NEWTONGRANGE Midlothian	SC
06 Sep 2015	SHAWFAIR Midlothian	SC
06 Sep 2015	STOW Midlothian	SC
06 Sep 2015	TWEEDBANK Selkirkshire	SC
26 Oct 2015	BICESTER VILLAGE (formerly Bicester Town) Oxfordshire	SE
26 Oct 2015	ISLIP Oxfordshire	SE
26 Oct 2015	OXFORD PARKWAY Oxfordshire	SE
13 Dec 2015	APPERLEY BRIDGE West Yorkshire	YH
13 Dec 2015	CRANBROOK Devon	SW

2016 — 5 stations

18 Jan 2016	BERMUDA PARK Warwickshire	WM
18 Jan 2016	COVENTRY ARENA Warwickshire	WM
19 June 2016	KIRKSTALL FORGE Leeds	YH
16 May 2016	LEA BRIDGE London	LO
11 Dec 2016	EDINBURGH GATEWAY	SC

2017 — 3 stations

02 April 2017	ILKESTON Derbyshire	EM
02 April 2017	LOW MOOR Bradford	YH
21 May 2017	CAMBRIDGE NORTH Cambridge	EE

Chapter 11

Lines and chords by date

1969		21km
BARASSIE-KILMARNOCK	21km	May 1969

1971		24km
PETERBOROUGH-SPALDING	24km	07 Jun 1971

1975		32km
PERTH-LADYBANK	32km	06 Oct 1975

1976		3km
DERBY-SINFIN	3km	04 Oct 1976

1977		21km
LIVERPOOL UNDERGROUND LOOP AND NORTH-SOUTH LINES	5km	03 Feb 1977
LEAMINGTON SPA-COVENTRY	16km	02 May 1977

1979		8km
GLASGOW ARGYLE LINE	8km	05 Nov 1979

1982		1km
BLAENAU FFESTINIOG NORTH-BLAENAU FFESTINIOG	1km	22 Mar 1982

1983		34.5km
PENISTONE-BARNSLEY	11km	16 May 1983
DALSTON-STRATFORD	4.5km	17 May 1983
SELBY EAST COAST MAIN LINE DEVIATION	19km	03 Oct 1983

1984		22.5km
BLAYDON-DUNSTON-NEWCASTLE	6.5km	01 Oct 1984
BURNLEY-TODMORDEN	16km	01 Oct 1984

1985		8km
CARDIFF CITY LINE	8km	11 May 1985

1986   22.1km

BATHGATE-NEWBRIDGE JUNCTION (EDINBURGH)	16km	24 Mar 1986
ADDLESTONE-BYFLEET & NEW HAW CURVE	1km	12 May 1986
KENSINGTON OLYMPIA-WILLESDEN	4.5km	12 May 1986
STOCKPORT HAZEL GROVE CHORD	0.6km	12 May 1986

1987   51.9km

KETTERING-CORBY	8km	13 Apr 1987
Closed 04 Jun 1990, reinstated 23 Feb 2009		
OXFORD-BICESTER TOWN	16km	09 May 1987
COVENTRY-NUNEATON	16km	11 May 1987
ROTHERHAM CENTRAL Junction-ALDWARKE Junction	3km	11 May 1987
HEYSHAM-MORECAMBE	6.5km	11 May 1987
ROTHERHAM HOLMES CHORD LINK	1.2km	11 May 1987
BIRMINGHAM SNOW HILL to MOOR STREET reinstatement	1.2km	05 Oct 1987

1988   16km

FARRINGDON-BLACKFRIARS (Snow Hill Tunnel) reinstatement	1.5km	16 May 1988
Route on which passenger trains last ran in 1916 and freight until 1969		
Reopened as part of Thameslink		
SALFORD CRESCENT-DEANSGATE (Windsor Link)	1km	16 May 1988
Curve allowing trains from Bolton and Preston to reach Manchester Piccadilly		
DIDCOT NORTH Junction-FOXHALL Junction	1km	16 May 1988
ABERDARE-ABERCYNON	11km	03 Oct 1988
LICHFIELD CITY-LICHFIELD TRENT VALLEY High Level	1.5km	28 Nov 1988

1989   29.5km

WALSALL-HEDNESFORD	16km	08 Apr 1989
TIMPERLEY-STOCKPORT	11km	15 May 1989
AIRDRIE-DRUMGELLOCH extension	2.5km	16 May 1989

1990   28km

SWINTON CURVE	1km	17 Mar 1990
SYSTON NORTH-EAST CURVE Leicester	1km	14 May 1990
BLACKBURN-CLITHEROE	16km	19 May 1990
GLASGOW-PAISLEY CANAL	10km	30 Jul 1990

1991   5.5km

STANSTED AIRPORT LINK (north and south curves)	5.5km	10 Mar 1991

1992   14.1km

INVERKEITHING NORTH-EAST CURVE	0.6km	05 Jan 1992

WAKEFIELD-PONTEFRACT . . . . 13.5km   11 May 1992

1993   49.6km

NOTTINGHAM-NEWSTEAD	17km	08 May 1993
MANCHESTER AIRPORT LINK	2.5km	17 May 1993
BRIDGEND-MAESTEG	13km	28 Sep 1993
RUTHERGLEN-WHIFFLET	11.5km	04 Oct 1993
COWLAIRS CHORD Glasgow	0.6km	Oct 1993
GLASGOW QUEEN STREET-MARYHILL	5km	06 Dec 1993

1994   55.1km

BRISTOL (N-E) LOOP	0.8km	29 May 1994
LIVERPOOL CURVE Earlestown	0.7km	29 May 1994
MITRE BRIDGE CURVE London	1.5km	29 May 1994
SHEEPCOTE LANE CURVE London	0.6km	29 May 1994
CHANNEL TUNNEL	50.5km	14 Nov 1994
WATERLOO CURVE/STEWARTS LANE VIADUCT	1km	14 Nov 1994

1995   14.5km

SNOW HILL-SMETHWICK WEST reinstatement	6.5km	24 Sep 1995
NEWSTEAD-MANSFIELD WOODHOUSE	8km	20 Nov 1995

1996   34.35km

MANCHESTER AIRPORT SOUTH CURVE	0.75km	15 Jan 1996
MIDDLESBROUGH-NORTHALLERTON	23km	20 Feb 1996
COATBRIDGE CENTRAL-GREENFAULDS	3.6km	27 May 1996
LINLITHGOW-DALMENY	7km	03 Jun 1996

1997   35.5km

CREDITON-OKEHAMPTON	29km	25 May 1997
HEDNESFORD-RUGELEY TOWN	6.5km	01 Jun 1997

1998   40.5km

MANSFIELD WOODHOUSE-WORKSOP	21km	24 May 1998
WALSALL-WOLVERHAMPTON	10km	24 May 1998
RUGELEY TOWN-RUGELEY TRENT VALLEY	1.5km	25 May 1998
HEATHROW AIRPORT Junction-HEATHROW TERMINAL 4	8km	23 Jun 1998

1999   8km

CUMBERNAULD-GREENHILL	8km	Sep 1999

2000   11km

HALIFAX-HUDDERSFIELD/SOWERBY BRIDGE-MIRFIELD . . .	11km	28 May 2000

2002   20.5km

PORTOBELLO JUNCTION-NEWCRAIGHALL	2.5km	03 Jun 2002
CWRT SART Jct-MORLAIS Jct (Swansea District Line)	18km	Jun 2002

2003   86.8km

DOLPHINGSTONE EAST COAST MAIN LINE DEVIATION . . .	1.8km	21 Apr 2003

*New route around Dolphingstone, which is between Wallyford and
Prestonpans, because of land subsidence*

DORE SOUTH CURVE	0.5km	May 2003
EASTLEIGH-ROMSEY	10.5km	18 May 2003
HIGH-SPEED 1 Phase 1	74km	28 Sep 2003

2005   37.2km

BARRY-BRIDGEND *Y Barri - Pen-y-bont ar Ogwr*	30.5km	12 Jun 2005
MARYHILL-ANNIESLAND	1.5km	29 Sep 2005
ALLINGTON CHORD near Grantham	0.5km	13 Oct 2005

To remove local trains from the East Coast main line

HAUGHEAD JUNCTION-LARKHALL	4.7km	12 Dec 2005

2007   39km

HIGH-SPEED 1 Phase 2	39km	14 Nov 2007

2008   56.7km

NEWPORT EBBW Juntion-EBBW VALE PARKWAY	29km	06 Feb 2008
HEATHROW TERMINALS 1 2 3-TERMINAL 5	1.7km	27 Mar 2008
STIRLING-ALLOA-KINCARDINE	21km	19 May 2008

Includes freight-only section from Alloa to Kincardine

AYLESBURY-AYLESBURY VALE PARKWAY	5km	14 Dec 2008

2009   24.7km

KETTERING-CORBY	8km	23 Feb 2009

Previously reopened 13 Apr 1987 to 04 Jun 1990

OLIVE MOUNT CHORD, Liverpool	0.4km	06 Mar 2009
CORBY-MANTON JUNCTION	16km	27 Apr 2009
SYSTON EAST Junction-SYSTON NORTH Junction	0.3km	27 Apr 2009

2010 — 31.5km

DALSTON JUNCTION-NEW CROSS East London Line	9.5km	23 May 2010
AIRDRIE-BATHGATE	22km	12 Dec 2010

2011 — 2.2km

DALSTON JUNCTION-HIGHBURY & ISLINGTON	2.2km	28 Feb 2011
East London Line extension over existing North London Line route		

2012 — 3km

SURREY QUAYS-OLD KENT ROAD (for Clapham Junction)	1.5km	10 Dec 2012
East London Line link to existing South London line route		
NUNEATON NORTH CHORD	1.5km	15 Nov 2012

2013 — 2km

HITCHIN FLYOVER	2km	26 Jun 2013

2014 — 4.4km

IPSWICH BACON FACTORY CHORD	1.2km	24 Mar 2014
DONCASTER NORTH CHORD at Shaftholme	3.2km	3 Jun 2014

2015 — 56km

TODMORDEN CURVE	0.5km	17 May 2015
EBBW VALE PARKWAY-EBBW VALE TOWN	2.5km	17 May 2015
NEWCRAIGHALL(Edinburgh)-TWEEDBANK	49km	6 Sep 2015
(Borders Railway)		
BICESTER CHORD	1km	26 Oct 2015
YEOVIL JUNCTION to YEOVIL PEN MILL	3km	14 Dec 2015

2016 — 16km

NORTON BRIDGE CHORD	10km	29 Mar 2016
OXFORD PARKWAY-OXFORD	6km	11 Dec 2016

2017 — 6km

WAREHAM-NORDEN Swanage Railway	6km	13 Jun 2017

TEAMWORK: *Railwatch* editor Ray King with his daughter Eleanor (who helped produce the graphics for this book) at the opening of the Borders Railway. Picture by former *Railway Magazine* editor Nick Pigott

Many of the stations and lines opened in this book have been the subject of ideas and promotion by The Railway Development Society Limited, campaigning as Railfuture. It is an independent organisation with branches throughout Great Britain. We campaign for the development of our rail network for freight, passenger and light rail services as an essential part of a sustainable environment.

The Railway Development Society Limited   **www.railfuture.org.uk**

Why not join us? All members receive regular news magazines covering national and branch affairs including our quarterly magazine *Railwatch*. We publish booklets, organise conferences, hold meetings and other activities for members. You can photocopy the form at the back of this book or download one from our website at www.railfuture.org.uk.

Acknowledgements

Railfuture is grateful to its many members throughout Great Britain who have contributed information and photographs for this book. The assistance of Paul Abell, Chris Austin, John Bearpark, Philip Bisatt, Roger Blake, Ian Brown, Malcolm Bulpitt, Lloyd Butler, Mike Crowhurst, Peter Cousins, Nigel Cripps, Keith Dyall, Trevor Garrod, Mark Gleeson, Mike Harrison, Paul Jeffries, Elisabeth Jordan, Peter Kenyon, Eleanor King, Maggie King, Graham Larkbey, Donald MacPhee, Brian Morrison, Colin Nash, Nigel Perkins, Rowland Pittard, Adrian Shooter, Tony Smale, Roger Smith, Michael Stevenson, Mike Watson and Bruce Williamson is particularly appreciated.

Passenger numbers on Britain's railways continue to rise but investment in new trains and track isn't keeping up. Railfuture campaigns strongly for more investment in rail to make life easier for current and future passengers.

What we stand for

The development of a bigger and better railway that people are proud and pleased to use.

Railfuture campaigns for:

- value-for-money fares
- more seats and better on-board facilities
- more frequent, reliable services
- quicker, easier journeys
- more accessible trains and stations
- new services and lines
- shifting freight from road to rail

We campaign nationally and locally on rail issues that passengers care about through our branches and affiliated rail user groups. In pressing for better rail services, we take every opportunity to develop positive relationships with national and local politicians and government officials.

We meet rail companies frequently, gaining insights which help us to influence their investment and policies in favour of passengers. In our contacts with rail companies, the media and the public, ours is a powerful, independent voice that fearlessly speaks up for passengers. National and local government run formal consultations before making major policy decisions to find out what the public think about the issues. Our informed responses to these consultations are well respected and influence policy in a passenger-friendly way.

Before making major policy decisions, both national and local government run formal consultations to find out what the public think about the issues. Railfuture's realistic, informed responses to these consultations are well respected, so the rail user viewpoint is considered and we can influence those policy decisions.

SUCCESS!
In 50 years, more than 370 stations and 500 miles of route have been added to the network, meeting with tremendous popular support.

In 20 years, passenger numbers have doubled.

Delay Repay is already triggered after delays of only 15 minutes on some services. We are pressing for this to be extended to other services now.